At Issue

| Sexual Consent

Other Books in the At Issue Series

At Issue

| Sexual Consent

Martin Gitlin, Book Editor

Published in 2020 by Greenhaven Publishing, LLC
353 3rd Avenue, Suite 255, New York, NY 10010

Articles in Greenhaven Publishing anthologies are often edited for length to meet page
requirements. In addition, original titles of these works are changed to clearly present
the main thesis and to explicitly indicate the author's opinion. Every effort is made to
ensure that Greenhaven Publishing accurately reflects the original intent of the authors.
Every effort has been made to trace the owners of the copyrighted material.

Cover image: Gary Waters/Ikon Images/Getty Images

Library of Congress Cataloging-in-Publication Data

Names: Gitlin, Marty, editor.
Title: Sexual consent / Martin Gitlin, book editor.
Description: First edition. | New York : Greenhaven Publishing, 2020. | Series: At
issue | Includes bibliographical references and index. | Audience: Grades 9-12.
Identifiers: LCCN 2019022609 | ISBN 9781534506329 (library
binding) | ISBN 9781534506312 (paperback)
Subjects: LCSH: Sexual consent. | Sexual ethics. | Sex and law.
Classification: LCC HQ32 .S397 2020 | DDC 176/.4—dc23
LC record available at https://lccn.loc.gov/2019022609

Manufactured in the United States of America

Website: http://greenhavenpublishing.com

Contents

Introduction

It took famous people to make sexual consent a national issue. It became news when athletes and actors and politicians were accused of making unwanted sexual advances. The every-day people who had been subject to such attacks for centuries received little attention. And that was a terrible shame.

But the publicity generated by sexual abuse accusations against those in the public eye has brought a spotlight to the issue. People have begun talking about it. They have debated what constitutes sexual consent and what does not. Those judged to have attacked or even harassed others sexually have been punished. Men, who have created most of the problem, have started to talk about the rights and wrongs in their potential sexual relationships. And many of them are trying to learn how to behave with more consideration and courtesy.

The issue is a thorny one. The problem of sexual consent leads to many questions that might seem awkward but that must be answered. Some people argue that a proper approach to relationships with a potential sexual partner is just common sense. They state that no means no, plain and simple. But others believe it is more complicated. They assert that sometimes the word "no" is never spoken and that one would have to be a mind reader to know if a green light toward sexual activity is flashing.

There is indeed a lot of gray area in the discussion that revolves around the following questions: Where is the line drawn between flirting and sexual harassment? What constitutes consent? Once consent is mutually understood, what signals should be given by one partner that the other has gone far enough? Does the use of drugs or alcohol make potential victims any more vulnerable? Does provocative clothing worn by a woman make unwanted sexual advances or presumptions any more justified?

The issue of sexual harassment leaped into the spotlight in 1991. That is when law professor Anita Hill accused United States Supreme Court nominee Clarence Thomas of unwanted sexual advances. The charges resulted in nationally televised hearings in which Thomas denied any wrongdoing. His eventual confirmation to the highest court of the land angered millions of women who believed his guilt had been proven. They also felt his behavior toward Hill suggested that he would not judge women's issues fairly as a Supreme Court justice.

The Thomas case brought a higher level of awareness of how even suggestive sexual talk makes others uncomfortable and can be considered harassment. Once the issue had been thrust into the spotlight, many other incidents that involved the world of politics and entertainment followed. Athletes, singers, actors, and politicians—including President Donald Trump—were accused publicly of sexual harassment, assault, and even rape. Some lost their jobs. Others narrowly escaped. One of the most controversial cases was that of Brett Kavanaugh, another Supreme Court nominee, who was peppered with questions on national television in 2018 about accusations of attempted rape years earlier. He too was confirmed to the highest court in the land.

The Kavanaugh hearing raised another issue involving sexual impropriety. And that revolves around the unwillingness of victims to come forward after an incident, or the amount of time that lapses before charges are made. Many women who claim to have been victims of sexual harassment or assault have hesitated or declined to inform the authorities. Some have felt a sense of shame for what happened to them. Others fear retribution from the attacker. Still others question whether bringing charges will result in any punishment or justice. But many women throughout the world have encouraged victims to make their voices heard. The result was the birth of the #MeToo movement.

Meanwhile, what many believe to be the gray area of sexual consent continues to be discussed and debated. Some claim that potential partners receive mixed signals or even a green light toward sexual advancement. Some perceive a green light to be flashing all the way into the bedroom and do not read accurately when the light has changed to red. Others contend that a red light is easy to read. They assert that one does not need to say words such as "no" or "stop" to signal their discomfort over sexual activity.

What had been assumed for years is no longer assumed. Among those assumptions is that women wearing revealing and provocative clothing are more open to sexual advances than others. Or that they are inviting trouble by showing more skin, thereby whetting sexual appetites. But that has proven to be a fallacy. Women around the world have stated plainly that being sexual or dressing in a way that might be called provocative is no excuse for unwanted sexual suggestions or advances.

These issues are explored and answered in *At Issue: Sexual Consent*. The viewpoints that follow have been written by experts on the subject. They write about consent—when and how it is given and whether it can be reversed. They write about what constitutes sexual consent and unwanted sexual activity. They write about legal issues involving victims and perpetrators. They write about sexual harassment and assault on college campuses.

Once the issues surrounding sexual consent reached the spotlight, the subject seemed destined to remain there. One can assume they will stay in the news for decades to come. A time in which charges of sexual impropriety disappear certainly does not appear to be on the horizon. But greater awareness of what constitutes sexual consent, as well as a willingness to understand and heed the feelings of potential partners, will bring everyone to a safer place. Most people believe it will result in stronger and healthier relationships to all involved.

1

What Constitutes Consent?

Joseph J. Fischel

Joseph J. Fischel is associate professor of women's, gender and sexuality studies at Yale University. He is the author of Sex and Harm in the Age of Consent *(2016). His latest book is* Screw Consent: A Better Politics of Sexual Justice *(2019).*

Some forms of consent are obvious and clear. But others are trickier. What if deception is involved? Throughout history, people have misrepresented and lied about themselves in order to seem more attractive to potential sexual partners. If a person is deceived in such a way, is one's consent rendered illegitimate? The practice of trying to convince others to engage in sexual activity through lying and other deceptive means is touched on in the following excerpted article. The use of dishonesty and trickery to lure a potential partner to go along is among the issues of consent that have been growing as a topic of debate in recent years. But maybe an equally worthwhile question is why do so many women feel pressured into consenting in the first place.

[…]

Cases of alleged deception raise a surprisingly hard-to-answer question: what do we consent to when we consent to sex? Turned around, the question becomes: what kinds of deception or nondisclosure ought to be legally impermissible for procuring sex?

"What Do We Consent to When We Consent to Sex?" by Joseph J. Fischel, Aeon Media Group, 10/23/2018. https://aeon.co/ideas/what-do-we-consent-to-when-we-consent-to-sex. Licensed under CC BY-ND 4.0 International.

If consent separates rape from sex, as the US legal commentator Jed Rubenfeld put it in 2013, then we should be seriously concerned about all kinds of deception, nondisclosure, false advertising and so forth. If Debbie consents to sex with David because David lies that he is an atheist, rich, a Bernie bro, a Harvard alumnus, her husband, whatever—is not Debbie's consent vitiated? Is the sex rape?

Scholars such as Corey Rayburn Yung counter that these problems appear only in mythical doctrinal theory land and not in the real world of sexual coercion. Yet the conviction of trans and gender-nonconforming defendants belies that claim, and shows that the problem is a real one. There is a solution, in two parts.

First, we should render as a legal wrong, although not a crime, the deliberate contravention of an explicit conditional for the procurement of sex. The civil rights attorney Alexandra Brodsky makes a parallel argument about "stealthing," the nasty practice of removing a condom unbeknown to one's partner. So if Debbie says to David: "I will sleep with you if, and only if, you are Republican," and David lies about his political-party affiliation, the subsequent sex becomes legally wrongful. Yet rather than sentence David to prison (a typical penalty for a crime), we might obligate David to pay Debbie money or compensate her in some other way (a typical penalty for a tort violation).

Of course, sex rarely happens under such if-and-only-if conditions; yet tailoring the law like this means that we can keep consent as our metric of sexual assault rather than reverting to an archaic standard of force.

Second, it is important to understand that some questions are or should be unanswerable as legal truth claims. When it comes to sex, there should be no legally actionable way to answer the question: "Are you a man?" Is gender a matter of genitals, hormones, chromosomes, secondary sex characteristics, social inequality or self-identification? The law cannot bring any clear answer to this question. One should not be convicted of sexual assault for failing to live up to a phallocentric standard of manhood.

Yet rendering as a legal wrong, but not a crime, the deliberate contravention of an explicit conditional in order to procure sex intimates how crappy consent is as a metric for sexual ethics. It bears reminding that legal responsibility is not the same thing as moral responsibility. One could lie to a prospective partner that he is an unmarried and wealthy libertarian, when in fact he is a married and poor socialist. It does not mean that one should do so, even if the subsequent sex is legally consensual (lest the partner explicitly premised her consent on any or all of these marital, financial or political party statuses). Despite recent declarations of consent's sexiness and goodness, consent offers us little direction when it comes to sexual communication, misrepresentation or nondisclosure of facts about ourselves to our partners. Moreover, consent offers minimal guidance as to how we ought to behave at the bar, dance club or frat party. So don't grab Ben's or Jen's genitals without an indication of willingness from Ben or Jen. But what kinds of embellishments, flirtations, pressures or even lies can you peddle to Ben or Jen to pursue your ambition to sleep with them?

Consent has limits not just in terms of scope but also in terms of sufficiency and applicability.

As for sufficiency: if Peter requests that Adam remove his legs or cut off his face as part of their sexual encounter, are we prepared to say Adam's consent (affirmative consent!) absolves Peter of any legal or moral responsibility? If we are not, can our reservations simply be sourced to erotophobia (fear of sex)? I don't think so.

As for applicability: many people suppose that sex with nonhuman animals is wrong because animals cannot consent. But are animals really the kinds of creatures capable of consenting? Can Fido "consent" or not to fetch? If you do believe animals such as cows can proffer consent, I would wager they are less likely to consent to becoming a cheeseburger than to sex.

Finally, maybe consent is more often the problem than the solution to bad sex. Why do people, too often girls and women, consent to sex that is immiserating, painful, unwanted and unpleasant? What social, cultural and economic forces make consenting to awful sex less costly than saying no? Far from being solved by consent, that problem is constituted by it. Consent does not solve all our social problems or intimate injustices. Just like we consent to deadening jobs, we often consent to injurious sex. Right-wing talk show hosts decry that some in the #MeToo movement have confused rape with bad sex, but it's critical that we make bad sex, and not just rape, a primary target of our sexual politics. I don't mean bad sex as in mediocre sex … I mean sex that is persistently unwanted, or painful or begrudgingly acquiesced to, or requires illicit substances to endure.

Let's collaborate to create opportunities for intimacy and sexual satisfaction, particularly for people historically tasked with satisfying others rather than being satisfied themselves. Let's imagine a progressive sexual politics in which the sex that too many of us consent to is the problem, rather than the antidote.

2

Time to Bust the Myths Surrounding Sexual Violence

Serlo

Serlo offers intuitive explanations, courses, videos, exercises and sample solutions. Students can use these to learn according to their needs and at their own pace. The entire offer is completely free of charge and advertising.

This viewpoint presents a list of myths about sexual violence and breaks them down into truths. There are many common justifications people make when someone is the victim of sexual abuse, and the truth is, no one asks for it. No one deserves it. The victim is not to blame. The offender was not confused by gray areas. It's all pretty simple. Yet, these myths pervade.

1. People can consent to sex when they are intoxicated, asleep, under the effect of drugs, in a situation of danger.

As someone cannot verbally or physically affirm their desire to take part in a sexual activity when they are not conscious they (logically) can't consent. Even if they had consented earlier, or had consented a previous time, they cannot consent in that moment and therefore any sexual contact would be a crime.

"Myths Busted II: Yes, That Also Counts as Sexual Violence," Serlo. https://en.serlo. org/78364/myths-busted-ii-yes-also-counts-sexual-violence. Licensed under CC BY 4.0.

2. When someone gets drunk and they are sexually assaulted, it was their fault.

See above. No. Instigating sexual contact, of any kind, with someone who is not able to consent is never ok (and generally illegal). Someone's decision to get drunk does not change that fact. Alcohol consumption is legal in the United Kingdom, and in most European countries, for anyone over the age of 18, and people have the right to consume or not consume it as they see appropriate. Yet sexual assault and alcohol consumption are two very separate things: one does not negate the other, or excuse it, in anyway.

3. Touching people sexually without their permission, unwanted sexting, publishing their nude or sexual pictures or videos online is not abuse, it's just banter.

Online abuse has sadly become increasingly common and has nothing to do with fun and innocent banter. It is a violent and vilifying act, and, legally, a crime. Survivors of cyber-abuse often struggle with long-term mental health issues such as depression, anxiety, self-loathing and suicidal thoughts. If ever you survived any of these experiences, you are incredibly brave and resilient, and support is available for you.

4. Men cannot be sexually abused.

Unfortunately, people of any gender and sexual orientation can be, and are assaulted and abused. The assumption that "true men do not get themselves raped" is terribly harmful and makes the healing process of those self-identifying men who experienced sexual abuse even more challenging. Abuse is never the abused person's fault, and gender-based stereotypes truly damage us all.

5. There is no abuse in LGBT+ relationships. Women cannot abuse each other.

Sadly sexual abuse can happen in many different contexts and self-identifying women can abuse as well as men (even though male violence on women currently counts for a great part of sexual assault cases). This means it is vital to understand and practice consent in any kind of relationship.

6. Assault only happens in dark streets at night. One can only be assaulted by strangers.

Most cases of assaults today happen in a domestic context, and the assaulter is someone the abused person knew. Too many survivors take years to realise that what they went through (for example, being forced into unwanted sex by an ex-partner) was a form of sexual abuse. Importantly, no abuse or assault is more or less serious or damaging than another, and all survivors need to be taken seriously and deserve the utmost support.

7. A sexual abuse that, for whatever reason, is not persecuted in a court is not real.

Sexual assault is a crime, and a serious one. However, some cases of sexual violence are difficult to persecute in court: perhaps because they happened a long time ago, the abuser was under-age, or evidence difficult to produce. The legal notion of assault varies from country to country, and some survivors also prefer not to go through the painful, and expensive, experience of a trial.

Again, they deserve everyone's respect and support whatever their choice. While it is our duty to build a fair legal system and a healthy consent culture to tackle sexual violence in our society, we should remember that assaults that are not persecuted in the court are nonetheless real and a profoundly traumatic experience. So are sexual encounters that may not qualify as assaults under a country's legislation, but entail lack of consent from one side.

8. Sexual assault can be blamed on what the assaulted person was wearing.

Sexual violence has little to do with sexual attraction, and much to do with power and control. Men (or anyone, for that matter) cannot be "provoked" or "lured" into assaulting someone. People of every gender and sexual orientation, race and class get violated, in different times and spaces and independently of what they were wearing. This is a terrible truth we need to change by building a healthy culture of consent. Which starts by understanding that no abuse is EVER, on any account, the abused person's fault.

9. If you bring someone back with you from a night out you're giving them the green light for sex. If you make that decision you should deal with the consequences (aka: you can't share a bed with someone and NOT have sex. That's just impossible.).

We'll repeat it again. And again. Sexual partners should consent freely to ANY activity they engage in. Going back home with someone, or sleeping in the same bed, does not mean we are consenting to sex, even if that person is our long-term romantic partner. And consenting to a certain sexual practice does not mean consenting to others, or that we'll always do so. People ALWAYS have the right to say no, change their mind, and stop at any moment.

10. Sex in a relationship is never abusive.

Sadly even people who love us, or say they do, can harm us and violate our physical, sexual and emotional boundaries. Long-term partners, in the context of heterosexual as well as LGBT+ relationships, can be sexually abusive. This include forcing or pressuring their partners into any kind of unwanted sexual activities with themselves or others, and sharing sexual pictures or videos of them without their consent. Love never justifies violence or abuse, and, unfortunately, abusive partners tend to be recidivists (return to the abusive behavior multiple times). Many forms of support are available for those who wish to come out of abusive relationships, and techniques to learn to understand and communicate with our partners regarding our sexual and emotional needs can be learned (look at our piece on how to express/identify consent!).

11. Being sexually abused is shameful for the abused person.

Most emphatically not. Abusing, raping, assaulting is shameful and criminal behavior. On the contrary, surviving any of the above means you went through something terrible, but have been brave, resilient and strong enough to survive. Nothing of what happened to you was ever your fault.

12. It is OK to pressure LGBTQ+ people into heterosexual sex to "make them normal."

There is a common misconception that peope's sexual orientation can be changed or "normalised," or that people can be "turned" by sex. This is not the case. For many LGBTQ+ people, it can feel like everyone is expected to be straight. A 2012 survey by the Human Rights Campaign found that 92% of LGBTQ+ teens had heard negative things about being lesbian, gay, bisexual, or transgender, and the pressures to conform to a certain set of heteronormative parameters undoubtedly feed into this uneasiness.

It is never ok to pressure anyone, regardless of their sexual orientation, into an act they are not comfortable with. And it is wrong to try and change someone who experiences desires or attractions that are completely normal and personal to them.

3

Gray Area in Black and White

Reina Gattuso

Reina Gattuso is a columnist for the website Feministing, which is run by young feminists and features relevant topics in pop culture and politics. She is passionate about empowering conversations around queerness, sexual ethics, and social movements with equal parts rhapsody and sass. Her writing has appeared at Time, Bitch, attn:, *and* The Washington Post. *She is currently pursuing her masters degree.*

This viewpoint questions the notion of "gray area" in sexual consent. What is lived in reality may not easily translate to clinical language or the language of law. But the "gray area" also has been used throughout history to dismiss women's claims of harassment or assault, or to justify improper behavior. In this viewpoint, the author claims that it can be used as an excuse to encourage unwanted sexual activity or even to engage in abuse. The feeling is that the intentions of potential sexual partners are generally made quite clear and anything less than an obvious green light constitutes harassment or sexual violence.

If you've ever made a formal complaint of gendered violence, you might have felt that translating raw experience into the language of law is like describing a walk through the forest using only the formal scientific names of the trees. Whereas in lived

"Is There a 'Gray Zone' in Consent?" by Reina Gattuso, Feministing, May 2018. Reprinted by permission.

reality, you saw the sunlight filtered green through the leaves, noted the precise shine off a beetle's shell, and started at the sudden call of a bird, in telling it everything becomes technical, different. Whereas in lived reality, you were muddling through your discomforts, trying to use the right language to send the right signals, sometimes not sure what you wanted, the law is black and white. Did a sexual assault happen or didn't it happen? Is there evidence?

It's hard to translate the complexities of power, intimacy, and sexuality into a cohesive narrative for our own understanding, let alone to lodge a formal complaint. The schemas that feminists write in anti-domestic violence or sexual harassment pamphlets can seem simple, neat renditions of power and violence on the page, but when we look at some of our own experiences we may find them complex.

This complexity has been described by some as the "gray zone," or the idea that there is a space between consent and non-consent. Katie Roiphe opined on the concept in her 1993 book *The Morning After*, in which she argued that college campus feminists' activism against rape infantilized women by redefining ambiguously coercive sexual encounters as rape. Roiphe has continued to argue that contemporary feminists' widening of the definition of rape is a puritanical infantilization of women in the guise of progressive politics. Laura Sessions Stepp, meanwhile, popularized the idea in her 2007 *Cosmopolitan* article about "gray rape," or young women's ambiguous experiences of assault or sexual coercion, often involving alcohol.

But there's one problem: The "gray zone" idea has often functioned as a tactic to minimize or dismiss violence, and therefore evade accountability, by claiming that sex is inherently a murky, illegible realm.

Feminists on the other side of the debate respond to this by saying that consent is, after all, quite simple: It's a freely-given, enthusiastic "yes" which is clearly and unambiguously signaled, as simple as figuring out whether or not someone wants tea.

I've used this consent-is-black-and-white line in my own work. And yet a dissonance remains. Just as the translation of sexual violence or harassment from lived experience to legal complaint can reveal those aspects of experience that remain fraught and ambiguous in our own minds, our experiences of gender, power, and violence are not always black and white. That is not to say that all experiences of sexual violence are somehow elusive or ambiguous; there are plenty of clear and egregious instances of violence in which the idea of the "gray zone" is a strategy used to sow doubt in the minds of victims.

But in many of our lived experiences, there is complexity. Perhaps an experience involves multiple kinds of intersecting power—class, race, sexuality, gender—or takes place in the context of an intimate relationship with power dynamics we can't quite parse. For many of us, the complexity may revolve around the question of enthusiastic consent: Did I or my partner indicate it clearly enough?

These tensions recently came into relief in the discussion surround[ing] the Babe story on Aziz Ansari, a tale of a night of "bad sex" or sexual assault that is unsettling, yet ubiquitous. Feminist analyses of the incident emphasized that it was precisely the banality of the story that prompted pushback. If we admit that this is assault, many writers argued, we must reinterpret many of our own experiences, and that scares us; it means uprooting what we understand about intimacy, each other, ourselves. The more unflinching a gaze we turn to the violence of our own gender norms, the more we understand that coercion itself is a continuum.

There is a distinction, however, between acknowledging the complexity of gendered violence, and endorsing the idea that consent is an unknowable "gray zone." Because power is multilayered, advocates of the "gray zone" logic argue, we can shrug consent off as an inherently flawed framework and accept that some degree of coercion [is] inalienable to sex. But when we think of gendered violence as complex, moments of ambiguity or discomfort don't lead us to reject the responsibility of consent.

They rather push us to ask deeper questions about how gender and power shape our intimacies and how consent itself is enabled or hindered by power relations. Experiences that feel violating yet ambiguous challenge us to think of violence as a spectrum of power and coercion, rather than a simple dichotomy between "good sex" and "rape."

Katie Roiphe argues as much herself, albeit with the wrong conclusion, in her 2011 *New York Times* article, "In Favor of Dirty Jokes and Risque Remarks":

> *The so-called rape epidemic on campuses is more a way of interpreting, a way of seeing, than a physical phenomenon. It is more about a change in sexual politics than a change in sexual behavior . . . We all agree that rape is a terrible thing, but we no longer agree on what rape is . . . The lines between rape and sex begin to blur.*

Roiphe is right: It's not that suddenly, more people are being sexually harassed or sexually assaulted. It's that we're now labelling a lot of experiences as sexual violence when we didn't previously understand them as such. And it's true: That creates uncertainty about the meaning of rape, and of gendered violence more generally, and calls into question the "normal" idea of sex.

But here's where I (and many of us) differ from Roiphe, and it's a big difference. Whereas she takes the expanding definition of violence to indicate a society of puritanical paranoia, we take it to indicate a serious and important interrogation, in which violent gender norms can be revealed, reevaluated, and changed. This interrogation calls for us not only to expand our idea of violence, but to expand our critique of norms around gender and sexuality in general. If it is a normal experience for women to feel violated during sex, there is something wrong with "normal" sex. That doesn't mean all patriarchal sex is rape. That doesn't mean all sex which is uncomfortable, violating, or even coercive can be or should be criminal. That does mean we have to expand not only what we consider sexually violent, but how we respond to sexual violence.

If we understand sexual violence as necessarily committed against an innocent woman by an evil man who must be punished with years of jail time—then yes, it will be difficult for many of us to understand our own, daily experiences of violation as rape or assault. When we understand sexual violence as a coercive violation of someone's bodily autonomy which is enabled by social power imbalances—which can be addressed through multiple processes of justice—we give ourselves the space to articulate our own experiences in all their complexity.

I don't think consent is always simple. Power and intimacy are as complex as we are, and at the end of the day human intimacy is more fraught than tea time. But that doesn't mean that consent is a useless framework, that sex occurs in some amoral "gray zone," or that we're somehow off the hook for ensuring that our own encounters are enthusiastically consensual. It means, rather, that when we acknowledge the complexity of our lived experiences of power and violence, we find that creating genuine sexual equality requires much more than firing a few men or sending them to jail (though these things can be important). It requires the creation of a new normal.

4

To Confuse with Drugs and Booze

Alex Aldridge and Adam Winstock

Alex Aldridge is a PhD candidate at the University of London, researching sex, drugs and sexual consent. Her work focuses specifically on the contexts in which intoxicated sexual activity takes place, exploring the roles of space, the body, and how these interact with broader structural factors to shape consent practices. Adam Winstock is an Honorary Clinical Professor at the Institute of Epidemiolgy and Health Care, University College London. He is a Consultant Addiction Psychiatrist and Addiction Medicine specialist based in London. He has published over 120 papers, and he is the founder and director of Global Drug Survey, which runs the biggest drug survey in the world.

The authors of this viewpoint admit that determining sexual consent is complicated by drugs and alcohol. What can be perceived before and after sexual activity can sometimes be debated when memories are blurred by mind-altering substances. But sometimes drugs are taken by both parties to enhance the sexual experience. Among their claims is that consent must be discussed and negotiated with clarity by both sides before sexual activity takes place. Still, more must be understood about sexual consent, particularly intoxicated consent, and outreach efforts like the Global Drug Survey are a good place to start.

S exual consent is an important, complex and often awkward topic to talk about. And when people have been consuming alcohol or other drugs, it makes negotiating sexual consent even more complicated. Indeed, drawing the line between consensual sex and assault when a complainant is heavily intoxicated is a particularly difficult area of law.

What is clear though, is that context matters. The gender of the people having sex, their sexuality, the nature of their relationship and how they became intoxicated—whether willingly or unwillingly—all shape the judgements that we make about intoxicated consent.

The importance of context was brought to the forefront in the late 1970s and early 1980s, when the so-called "feminist sex wars" divided Western academics who were interested in gender equality. The debates were dominated by arguments over pornography and sex work, but the issue of sexual consent—and what it means for women living in a patriarchal society—was always present.

Context and Consent

Influential legal scholar Catharine MacKinnon drew attention to society being organised in such a way that men hold the power; women's consent and sexuality is, to some extent, conditioned and controlled by these power structures. MacKinnon's contemporary, Andrea Dworkin, took this argument further. She claimed that women's subordination underpins male sexual desire.

So, to give and receive consent meaningfully, there needs to be an awareness of the power dynamics at play, and the impact they have on the relationships among people. This raises questions about just how meaningful women's sexual consent can be under patriarchy. When women are not on an equal footing with men, are they really "free" to make choices about sex with those men?

Others have highlighted the role that sexuality plays in shaping mainstream views about sexual consent. For example, anthropologist Gayle Rubin has argued that historically, sexual consent has been a privilege afforded only to those who engage in socially accepted (or even socially encouraged) sexual behaviour—that is, heterosexual, monogamous, procreative sex. In the UK, as recently as 1997, the age of consent was higher for same sex sexual activity than it was for heterosexual sex. So, even if individuals were freely choosing such sexual activity, their consent was not legally recognised.

Assumptions around gender and sexuality also affect the way people think about intoxicated sexual consent today. For example, consider the public response to the so-called chemsex phenomenon: chemsex refers to the intentional use of drugs—often methamphetamine, GHB and mephedrone—to enhance and prolong sexual encounters between men who have sex with men.

Chemsex has largely been portrayed as a public health crisis, with an emphasis on the potential for the transmission of HIV. Yet little attention is paid to the sexual violence and exploitation men might well experience in chemsex settings. By contrast, when chemsex is discussed in relation to heterosexual people, the issue of sexual consent moves to the forefront.

A Worldwide Survey

It's useful to reflect on how categories such as gender and sexuality—and indeed race, ability and social class—might affect the way intoxication and sexual consent are talked about and understood. But while these categories are important, they are not enough to explain why certain intoxicated sexual experiences are perceived by those involved as consensual, and others not.

Based on an earlier project, for which Aldridge spoke with a diverse group of people who had had sex on drugs, it seems that in order to understand the complexity of intoxicated consent, it's necessary to probe further into the specific contextual elements of sex on drugs. That might include the settings in which this activity takes place (sex club, house party, music festival), the type of drug being consumed (MDMA, cannabis, alcohol) and the nature of relationship between those having sex (one-night stand, long-term relationship, group sex).

Intoxicated consent can be negotiated successfully, but understanding how these other contextual factors affect sexual relationships is vital to addressing situations where it's not. At present, only a fraction of sexual assault incidents are reported and even fewer result in convictions.

In 2013, the Global Drug Survey began to explore people's experiences of intoxicated sexual consent. Out of 22,000 people, 20% reported having had been taken advantage of while intoxicated, while 5% said that this had happened in the last year. What's more, 14% reported that they had been given drugs or alcohol by someone who intended to take advantage of them.

This year, the Global Drugs Survey is delving deeper. Researchers will be collecting contextual information from people who have been taken advantage of while intoxicated, including where they were, who they were with, their relationship with the person or people who took advantage of them and the type of drug they were using.

Cultural norms and tolerance for such behaviours vary between countries. Because the 2019 survey is translated into 22 languages, researchers will be able to compare outcomes across regions. The aim of this survey is to give a voice to those unable to speak out. The findings will be used to shape interventions that minimise harm and maximise support for people who have experienced sexual assault, while ensuring that perpetrators are correctly identified, and held responsible.

5

Shouldn't No Really Mean No?

Molly Redden

Molly Redden wrote this viewpoint when she worked as a reporter for the Guardian U.S. *She is currently a senior reporter at* HuffPost. *Her writing also has appeared in* Mother Jones *and* The New Republic.

Maybe we can all agree that "no means no," but what if that "no" occurs when consent is withdrawn, that is, indicated in the middle of the sexual act? Recent rape cases highlight a legal loophole resulting from a 1979 state supreme court ruling, prompting a renewed campaign for change. This viewpoint focuses on a case of an older North Carolina teenager, an alleged victim of rape, who had at first consented to sex but changed her mind when it became clear that her partner had grown violent. The author rails against the legal system of that state that disallows people to withdraw consent once it has been given.

One Monday in January, Aaliyah Palmer, 19, spent several hours telling law enforcement in Fayetteville, North Carolina, that she had been raped.

Things started out OK, she said, in a consensual encounter in a bathroom. But when the man having sex with her began tearing out her hair, she demanded he stop; he didn't.

"'No Doesn't Really Mean No': North Carolina Law Means Women Can't Revoke Consent for Sex," by Molly Redden, Guardian News and Media Limited, June 24, 2017. Reprinted by permission.

It was here a detective interrupted Palmer's account with a question. At any time after she said no, did her attacker stop having sex with her, then penetrate her once again?

Yes, Palmer said.

"OK," the detective replied, according to Palmer. "That's important."

It was important because in North Carolina, a person cannot withdraw consent for sex once intercourse is taking place. Because of a 1979 state supreme court ruling that has never been overturned, continuing to have sex with someone who consented then backed out isn't considered to be rape.

"The whole thing is ridiculous," Palmer told the *Guardian*. "It's crazy."

The North Carolina law is an example of how the US legal system has not always kept pace with evolving ideas about rape, sex and consent. Just last year, an Oklahoma court ruled that the state's forcible sodomy statute did not criminalize oral sex with a victim who is completely unconscious. The toughest charge available to prosecutors was unwanted touching.

But the North Carolina law appears to be unique. And it has shocked even those who are used to dealing with such legalistic vagaries.

"It's absurd," said John Wilkinson, a former prosecutor and an adviser to AEquitas, a group which helps law enforcement pursue cases of sexual violence. "I don't think you could find anyone today to agree with this notion that you cannot withdraw consent. People have the right to control their own bodies. If sex is painful, or for whatever reason, they have the right to change their mind."

The ruling has devastated victims and frustrated prosecutors in North Carolina for years. State senator Jeff Jackson, who has introduced legislation to amend the law, encountered a similar case when he was a criminal prosecutor. His office was ultimately forced to dismiss the rape charge.

"North Carolina is the only state in the country where no doesn't really mean no," he said in a statement. "We have a clear ethical obligation to fix this obvious defect in our rape law."

This May, another North Carolina woman, Amy Guy, revealed that the law had prevented prosecutors from charging her husband with rape, after a violent attack in which she repeatedly resisted.

Guy was estranged from her husband when he showed up unannounced at her new home and demanded she sleep with him. Her husband had been violent in the past, Guy said, so she consented. When he began to hurt her, she told him to stop. He did not.

A rape conviction could have carried a prison sentence of five and a half to nearly seven years, according to Guy's attorney. But once somebody in the prosecutor's office recalled the 1979 ruling, law enforcement allowed Guy's husband to plead guilty to a lesser charge, of misdemeanor assault, for being violent during their encounter.

"I was devastated," Guy said in an interview. "That did not make any sense. I was taught that no means no and it's not really true."

He was given a sentence of 10 months and is due to be released in November.

"No One Can Seriously Defend This Loophole"

The 1979 ruling, *State v Way*, arose after a man named Donnie Leon Way appealed his recent conviction for second-degree rape. Way was convicted of using extreme violence to force an acquaintance to submit to rape and oral sex. Wilkinson, the AEquitas adviser, said he was confounded as to why the state supreme court even introduced the idea of withdrawing consent.

"No one can seriously defend this loophole," Jackson said in his statement. His bill would amend state law to read, in part: "A person may withdraw consent to engage in vaginal intercourse in the middle of the intercourse, even if the actual penetration is accomplished with consent and even if there is only one act of vaginal intercourse …

"A defendant who continues the act of vaginal intercourse after consent is withdrawn is deemed to have committed the act of vaginal intercourse by force and against the will of the other person."

The proposal is stuck in committee with no sign that lawmakers will try to pass it before the current legislative session ends.

Palmer's case, however, has put the decades-old ruling back in the spotlight.

The person she says attacked her has not been arrested or charged. Palmer wonders if that is because it would be difficult to prove he penetrated her multiple times, after she told him to stop. In his defense, she reasons, he could say she consented at the beginning of intercourse and they only had sex once.

A Fayetteville police spokesperson did not respond to a message asking if the 1979 ruling had any influence on law enforcement's decision not to bring rape charges. Police have told Palmer and the *Fayetteville Observer*, which first publicized her case, that the evidence they collected wasn't enough to substantiate a rape.

Palmer agreed to be identified by name to create awareness of her case.

On a Saturday in January, according to Palmer and court documents, she and a friend went to Fort Bragg to connect with men they met on Tinder Social. After Palmer and her friend split up, Palmer went to a party in an apartment complex where she met the man she identifies as her assailant.

In an emptier apartment, she recalled, he pulled her into a bathroom to have sex. But when he began to grab her hair so hard that she could feel it ripping out, she told him he was hurting her and he had to stop. He told her to be quiet and relax, Palmer said. He didn't stop.

Palmer said she repeated her demand several more times, but he never relented. Fighting back seemed dangerous: "Army guys are trained in physical combat," she said.

During the ordeal, she said, she saw at least one camera phone that had been slipped under the bathroom door, apparently to make a recording. Four soldiers stationed at Fort Bragg were later charged with creating or possessing video recordings of the incident.

The following Monday, Palmer submitted to a rape kit and gave police the clothes she had worn that night.

But Fayetteville police did not charge the man Palmer says raped her. Palmer believes they waited too long to collect vital evidence. Between the time she reported a crime and the time investigators entered the apartment where she says the attack took place, she said, a week elapsed.

Since then, Palmer has become too depressed and anxious to go to class. Videos of her encounter circulated on Snapchat, and she is tortured by the thought that classmates might have seen them.

This spring, she withdrew from North Carolina State University, and she has lost at least one of her two scholarships because she is no longer a full-time student. She has also lost friendships.

"It was really heartbreaking for me," she said. "Everyone just believes that women are lying about rape … I'm going public about this to say, my word should be enough to be believed."

6

The Clarity of Consent

Alison Saunders

Alison Saunders is a British barrister and former Director of Public Prosecutions. She was the Chief Crown Prosecutor for CPS (Crown Prosecution Service) London when she wrote this viewpoint but has since stepped down.

This viewpoint focuses on the perceived and literal differences between victimization of rape and other crimes in society. The author criticizes the blame that is often placed on those who have been victims of a sexual crime. After all, victims of murder or fraud are not questioned or blamed for the crimes perpetrated against them. In Britain, a campaign initiated by the Crown Prosecution Service focuses on cases where two adults know each other, where consent might be perceived as murky. Some of the myths that surround sex offenses must also be debunked.

Consent Is ... beautiful, it is enthusiasm, it is free choice, it is mutual. It is NOT assumed, NOT a right of marriage, NOT in the clothes you wear.

These views, shared on Twitter this week in response to a new awareness campaign by the Crown Prosecution Service, which I head, show that the vast majority of people fully understand consent. And yet a myth persists that establishing whether

"Sexual Consent Is Simple. We Should All Be Clear What Constitutes Rape," by Alison Saunders, Guardian News and Media Limited, September 23, 2015. Reprinted by permission.

someone is a willing sexual partner is somehow complicated, even unreasonable.

Some victims are still blamed in a way that simply does not happen for other crimes. If someone is burgled, the automatic response is not to ask: "What did you do to deserve that?" If someone has their car stolen they haven't, historically, been expected to go through their car ownership history to see if the theft could be blamed on some "inadequacy" in their own behaviour to mitigate the guilt of the thief.

The issue is that for too long as a society we too have blamed victims—usually women—for letting themselves be raped; and we have forgiven perpetrators—usually men—for acting on some kind of instinct from which they seemingly must be protected.

This is insulting to both men and women, who in the vast majority of cases conduct affectionate, consensual, mutually agreeable relationships. The law is clear, and has been since 2003, that if one person does not consent to sexual activity, with the freedom and capacity to give that consent—and the other person doesn't reasonably believe there is consent—then it is an offence. Of course it is the job of the Crown Prosecution Service to prove this in court.

Capacity means that someone who is under severe influence of drink or drugs; someone who may be young or have certain learning disabilities; or who is asleep, may not be able to consent to sex. Freedom means that someone under pressure—for instance, within an abusive relationship or under pressure from someone in a position of trust (like a teacher, doctor, priest), or power (like an employer, gang leader, prison officer) may also not be considered to have freely consented.

It is only a decade ago that the criminal justice system, as well as the care system, was effectively turning its back on vulnerable girls who were being groomed for sex in many of our city centres. We now properly recognise that as rape. But then, few people understood that the very vulnerabilities that made the rapists target those girls—drink, drugs, unstable backgrounds—were the ones we mistakenly used to excuse their attackers. Many of us thought that no jury would believe these girls who craved attention and went back for more. But since then we have seen successful convictions across the country, and we have seen a change in attitude.

But the issue remains less well understood when the situation is between two adults who know each other. I want that to change for a number of reasons.

First, it is my job to apply the law and bring prosecutions. If people do not understand the law they will not understand why prosecutors are in our courts with increasing numbers of sex offences—they now make up more than 30% of crown court trials.

While criminal cases where consent is the issue may be complex to prosecute and difficult to prove that does not mean that the basic concept of consent itself is difficult. And that is the second reason—I want people to feel comfortable that they know when they might be a victim of crime, or a suspect of crime. We should all know where we stand.

In our campaign we have used a clever animation that compares sexual consent to having a cup of tea. You wouldn't force or pressure someone into having a cup of tea, and you can tell when someone wants a cup of tea or not. If someone says they want a cup of tea one minute, they can change their mind the next and should not be pressured to drink the tea. If this sounds simple, then so is the issue to consent to sex.

If you haven't seen it, I suggest you watch this film and join the #ConsentIs … debate. And I would just like to end by addressing some recent myths and misunderstandings that I think are damaging if they are left unchecked. I use genders in the below examples, but I fully acknowledge that both men and women can be both perpetrators and victims of sexual offences.

1. Men Now Have to Prove That They Got Consent

No. There has been no change in the law—the prosecution has to prove that consent was not given, but in considering that we will, of course, consider what made someone, for instance, reasonably believe that such consent was given. Similarly we will consider what made the woman consider that consent was not given. This is not in any way a change in the burden of proof. That remains with us.

2. Men and Women Are Treated Differently Because a Man Will Be Prosecuted for Having Sex When He Is Drunk Whereas a Woman Is Treated as a Victim

No. Gender is not a deciding factor. This has been discussed publicly as if it is clear cut—and I have read hundreds of these cases and they are never straightforward. I think there is an assumption that the authorities consider men the suspects and women the victims—that is not true, and is offensive to both genders. Each case is different.

3. A Woman Can Change Her Mind After the Event

No. The circumstances we consider will look at what made a suspect think that consent was given at the time. I think there is confusion here about the freedom and capacity to consent. In grooming cases, for instance, we have seen victims who did not realise that the pressure they were put under meant that they had not freely consented to sex. Evidence suggests that false rape claims are extremely rare.

4. Prosecutors Will Believe Anything That a Complainant Tells Them—and Will Prosecute on the Word of That Complainant Alone

No. We should always look at all the circumstances of a case so that as full a picture as possible can be gathered. Where, in the past, it seems to me that an over-suspicious or sceptical view of complainants' accounts pervaded, we now approach these cases without judgment, prejudice or preconceptions.

7

It's More Than Just a Yes or No Question

Dr. Lauren Rosewarne

Dr. Lauren Rosewarne is a senior lecturer in the School of Social and Political Sciences at the University of Melbourne, Australia. She currently teaches in the areas of political science and gender studies and writes, comments and speaks on a wide variety of topics including gender, sexuality, public policy, social media, pop culture and technology. She is the author of nine books, as well as journal articles, book chapters, and hundreds of opinion pieces and popular culture columns.

Consent is more complicated than a catchphrase or rallying cry. It would be much easier if "no means no" were all it took to avoid sexual harassment or abuse, but the truth is, our culture does not empower everyone to say "no" and have that assertion be respected and obeyed. The discussion needs to broadened. While attempts at movements like affirmative consent are a step in the right direction, they might not meet with success until society acknowledges and corrects stereotypes about men's and women's attitudes about sex.

Conversations about consent need to move beyond a rehash of the 1970s' women's lib catchcry of "no means no." The third-wave feminist switch to "yes means yes" however, isn't without its own limitations.

Consent is complicated.

When hearts are racing, stopping to catch one's breath and ask, "are you okay with this?"—or, God forbid, clicking the "Yes" button on a consent app—is often the wrong kind of dampener. In discussing consent, we need to acknowledge the complexities of male-female relationships, of prevailing sexual norms and also question the practical application of slogans, beyond bumper-stickers and T-shirts.

The underlying principle of "no means no" is a good one. It gives gravitas to sex needing to be wanted for it to occur and for "no" to be meaningful enough to halt advances. Focusing on "no," however, has two problematic consequences. First, what is overlooked is that "no" won't always leave the lips of a person in an unwanted sexual situation. Second, the absence of "no" isn't the same thing as consent.

In a culture in which women have the burden of being nice, of being *acquiescent*, saying "no" isn't easy. In an intimate situation, saying "no" requires a belief that things will stop if the word gets said, that a "no" won't get steamrolled and that no negative repercussions or challenges will follow. In a situation of assault by a stranger, saying no—saying, in fact, *anything at all*—may be the furthest thing from a victim's mind. When overwhelmed, when *overpowered*, and when fear is potentially *paralysing*, saying no or debating whether a verbal protest will make a difference is likely less important than soliciting help or making an escape.

The best-case scenario is that everybody feels empowered to say "no" and that once "no" gets spoken everything unwanted stops. The problem however, is that if a word like "no" had true potency, we wouldn't have to keep talking about consent. Events like the University of Melbourne's Respect Week would be rendered unnecessary, and the scourge of sexual violence would be merely a talking point for historians.

The reality alas, is that we have a culture in which rape occurs—frequently—and where victims often question their complicity. Equally, we have a situation where perpetrators, sometimes even reasonably, claim they were under the impression that things were consensual because that one word they'd been taught to listen out for was left unsaid.

We need to broaden the discussion beyond a preoccupation with "no."

First, we need to understand that "no" is only one of the ways objection gets expressed. Reluctant body language, spoken excuses, apprehensiveness and a lack of active participation are each examples.

Second, we need to force ourselves to get better at reading people. In an intimate situation, rather than assuming that everything is fine until you're told otherwise, the focus instead should be on signs of *enthusiasm*. This means making sure your partner is not just going along with things, but that they actively *want* sex to transpire: that they are *enthusiastic* about it.

In the US, universities and some state governments such as California have devoted much energy to the concept of affirmative consent—to moving the discussion beyond "no means no" to a focus on both parties needing to *really really* want sex—that is "yes means yes." This concept is now widely woven into violence prevention conversations and, perhaps less successfully, into the production of smartphone apps such as Good2Go and We-Consent.

"Yes means yes" however, isn't a sexual violence panacea. The sex-positive ethos that yearns for both parties to have an amazing time under the doona is being championed within the very same culture in which strangling scripts around intercourse thrive. Despite the successes of feminism and of the sexual liberation movement, in practice, it is generally men who steer sexual proceedings and it is women who are either happily participating, putting a stop to things or, more troubling, having things done to their bodies against their desires.

A woman taking a lead role in sex and voicing her desires comes at a cost in our still-puritanical society. A woman with a vocal appetite for sex, a woman with partners aplenty on her resumé continues to be denounced as a slut. It is therefore, unsurprising that a little reluctance on her part often plays out in courtship rituals and is often not construed as dissent, but rather as an integral part of seduction, of a woman being taken.

In encouraging a woman to vocalise her "yes" and to be demonstrative of her sexual desires, we need to be mindful that society hasn't yet embraced this.

Sex is still invariably understood as something women give to—or give up for—men; that a woman owning her horniness isn't yet transpiring without cost.

For sex to occur, sure the absence of protest is crucial. But it's only the start of a set of complicated conversations. No means no, absolutely. And waiting to hear that enthusiastic "yes, yes, yes" is an excellent step. But pretending such words have authority in a world of unevenly distributed power and enduring, if old-fashioned, sexual mores, isn't helpful.

There's much more to this conversation than yesses, nos and slogans.

8

It's Not About What You Wear

UN Women

UN Women is the United Nations entity dedicated to gender equality and the empowerment of women. A global champion for women and girls, UN Women was established to accelerate progress on meeting their needs worldwide. UN Women supports UN member states as they set global standards for achieving gender equality, and works with governments and civil society to design laws, policies, programs and services needed to ensure that the standards are effectively implemented and truly benefit women and girls worldwide.

The inspiration for this viewpoint is a display in Thailand that features clothing worn at the time of a sexual assault—including sweatpants and overalls—to prove the point that what a woman wears should never be to blame for sexual harassment or sexual violence. The viewpoint cites the exhibition as part of a push in that country similar to the #MeToo movement in the United States, in which women are inspired to fight back against sexual violence. The hope is that this exhibition and other discussions surrounding sexual assualt will clear up common misconceptions surrounding the topic.

As countries around the world reassess their views and approaches to sexual violence, in Thailand an exhibition that showcases victims' clothing challenges the notion that women's

UN Women (2018), "Don't Blame the Clothes: Challenging the Misconceptions of Sexual Violence," article published on the Regional Office for Asia and the Pacific website on June 25, 2018. Reprinted by permission.

appearance and behaviour are to blame when they are assaulted and asks audiences to question the acceptance of sexual violence.

The exhibition will be on display at Siam Paragon, Bangkok, from 25 June to 1 July and at the Bangkok Art and Culture Centre, from 3 to 15 July. By displaying the clothing victims wore at the time of the assault—from sweat pants to overalls—the exhibition will challenge the misconception that women are to be blamed for rape and sexual assault. The exhibition will also feature photographs and other interactive elements to invite the audience to question the ideas that sexual violence is acceptable, shameful, that women are responsible, or should not be spoken about.

The exhibition, titled Social Power Exhibition against Sexual Assault, is part of the campaign #DontTellMeHowToDress, organized by the campaign founder Cindy Sirinya Bishop. Thailand's answer to the #MeToo movement, the #DontTellMeHowToDress campaign, is an initiative led by local celebrities and activists to challenge social attitudes around sexual violence and the treatment of victims.

"Sexual harassment and assault is a very big issue in our society, but it's an issue no one really talks about," said Sirinya Bishop, a well-known model and actress. "There are many myths, stereotypes and a culture of victim blaming when it comes to women who have been assaulted. Women who do report sexual harassment and violence tell us they need better support by friends, colleagues, families, and communities."

"The sexual harassment incidences that Women and Men Progressive Movement Foundation has been collecting since 2015 show that victims of sexual harassment are younger than they were in the past. Most of the perpetrators are family members and close friends," explained Associate Professor Apinya Wechayachai, Director of Women and Men Progressive Movement Foundation. "The news reports often blame sexual violence on alcohol and drugs. However, according to multiple research studies, the fundamental factor is with men's dominant attitudes and traditional perceptions of manhood. To end sexual violence, we need to engage with men and boys and empower women to break the myths.

A recent UN study, *The Trial of Rape: Understanding the Criminal Justice System Response to Sexual Violence in Thailand and Viet Nam*, found that there are widespread misconceptions around sexual violence. The study demonstrates that many police and justice officials believe common myths about sexual violence, such as, that sexual assault must result in visible injury if the incident truly happened without consent, and that sexual violence is usually perpetrated by a stranger. Too often, women do not seek help because when they do speak out, many feel blamed for the violence committed against them by the very people tasked with protecting them.

To challenge misconceptions around sexual assault, the #DontTellMeHowToDress campaign aims to debunk the myth that women should avoid dressing provocatively or exposing themselves to the risk of assault. It aims to bring sexual harassment and assault into a public discussion. This includes questioning the silence which does not hold perpetrators accountable for their actions and the common impulse to question the behaviour of the victim rather than the perpetrator of sexual violence.

"What makes the #MeToo movement unique and powerful is that it sheds light on women's experiences, it has given them space to speak out, be heard and be supported, and has led to perpetrators being held accountable. Ending the culture of silence around sexual harassment and sexual violence will happen when this is discussed openly and when victims can speak out and receive immediate support. These can be uneasy conversations to have, but they are essential," Anna-Karin Jatfors, Deputy Regional Director of UN Women Regional Office for Asia and the Pacific, remarked.

The Social Power Exhibition against Sexual Assault is the result of collaborative support from Cindy Sirinya Bishop, UN Women, Women and Men Progressive Movement Foundation Thailand, Thai Health Promotion Foundation, the Embassy of Canada, Ministry of Social Development and Human Security,

Dtac, True Corporation PCL, L'Oreal (Thailand) Co., Ltd, Do Did Done Co., Ltd, Rapinnipha Co., Ltd, White Cafe Co., Ltd, artists and social activists Nat Prakobsantisuk, Chamnan Pakdeesuk and Jirawat Sriluansoi.

Thai celebrities associated with the project include Methenee Kingpayome, Lalita Panyopas, Sinjai Plengpanich, Treechada Petcharat, Vatanika Patamasingh, Panissara Phimpru, Davika Hoorne, Ranee Campen, Aniporn Chalermburanawong, Chutimon Chuengcharoensukying, Phillip Thinroj, Ananda Everingham, Pakin Kumwilaisuk, Nariporn Inkawat, Maynart Nantakwang Ann Mitrchai, and Kan Kantathavorn.

9

An Enticing Outfit Is No Excuse

Dean Burnett

Dean Burnett is a doctor of neuroscience and author of The Idiot Brain *and* Happy Brain: Where Happiness Comes From, and Why, *books that explore the brain and the origins and genesis of individual happiness. He is author of the popular* Guardian *science blog "Brain Flapping."*

The persistent idea that a woman's outfit can make her responsible for her own assault has no basis in science. In this viewpoint, the author, a neuroscientist, argues that any arousal felt from the appearance of provocative clothing cannot legally or morally justify unwanted sexual advances. He also claims that the old stereotypes of men seeking sex with any willing partner and women only with those with an emotional attachment have been proven outdated and false. Thus, he believes that blaming the victims for wearing sexy outfits diverts attention from real issues associated with sexual consent.

Sterling work by undercover reporters for the *Financial Times* have caused a storm around the Presidents Club. Reports of their annual gala dinner involving horrific harassment of hostesses, paid (surprisingly little) to cater to the whims of rich powerful men under alarmingly draconian conditions have quickly caused the club to close.

"How 'Provocative Clothes' Affect the Brain—and Why It's No Excuse for Assault," by Dean Burnett, Guardian News and Media Limited, January 25, 2018. Reprinted by permission.

This is just the latest in a long line of scandals regarding men in powerful positions using them to abuse, harass and sexually manipulate women. The potent backlash to the Presidents Club revelations and the ongoing #MeToo movement suggest that we may be undergoing a long-overdue societal shift when it comes to sexual politics and interactions, especially with regard to men exploiting their power over women.

Better-qualified people than I can/will tackle the complex political and social ramifications of all this. But there's one classic stock argument that should be tackled: that women who are assaulted are somehow to blame, because of the way they're dressed. Often deployed by angry guys and right-wing contrarians looking for attention, this argument has also been invoked with the Presidents Club story, even though the hostesses were dressed according to strict instructions from the employers.

It's hardly a new concept, and the argument has been lampooned many times. Yet clearly, it persists. But, does it hold up under scientific scrutiny?

The argument rests on the conclusion that women can dress in a way that causes such a powerful sexual arousal response in a man, he's stimulated beyond the limits of his self-control. The woman made the decision to look like she does, the man didn't have any choice about becoming so aroused, so the fault lies with her.

Legally, this doesn't work at all. Regardless of how a woman's dressed, she retains autonomy; even if she desperately wants sex, it remains her decision regarding who she has sex with. Consent is still important, regardless of how confusing many (supposedly) find it.

Having said that, the law and human biology often don't match up. In the UK you can have sex at 16, but you can't watch it until you're 18. Doesn't make much sense, but there we have it. So, is it biologically possible for a typical man to be sufficiently aroused by the sight of woman that it overwhelms his restraint? To answer this, you need to look at exactly what's going on in the brain when we experience arousal.

We're still far from a thorough understanding, but current evidence suggests that arousal, or perhaps more accurately "desire," has many cognitive components, beyond the basic physical characteristics. We observe something, our prefrontal cortex—via links to the more fundamental emotional and reward systems—analyses it and determines if it's sexual in nature, and if so, if it is "sufficiently" sexual (eg we find some people sexy, but not others). If it is, our attention is directed towards it, and emotional and motivation processes are activated via our amygdala and anterior cingulate cortex respectively. It's incredibly complex in detail, but the neurological systems that regulate arousal and desire do indeed have many potent effects via important regions throughout our brains.

One thing that could be said to support the notion that men are vulnerable to being sexually aroused by appearance, is evidence that suggests male arousal is far more visual in nature than female arousal. It does seem that the old stereotypes about men having less sophisticated sexual desires than women (men like porn, women like erotica etc) has some basis in fact. Some might argue that this is because males have evolved to "spread their seed" with whoever is available and desirable, whereas females, who do all the childrearing, evolved to look for more complex, enduring qualities in a partner, beyond just visual characteristics. Of course, this explanation relies on only one half of our species evolving to be monogamous (pair bonding, in scientific parlance). That seems … unlikely. Maybe the whole notion is just reverse engineered from modern stereotypes? Who can say.

There are more plausible explanations for this gender-asymmetry. Perhaps it's due to the different sex-hormone makeup? Or maybe it's a result of the fact that our sexual desires and the systems that support them develop along with the rest of our brain, so are influenced by the world around us. And in the world around us, the sexualised female form features so often in almost every medium that it's essentially a type of punctuation. You could argue that the reason men have a stronger visual element to their sexual arousal is because we live in a world where sexy images for men to see are everywhere, whereas women have tended to need to be more creative, and the brain develops accordingly. Perhaps this is changing too, what with women now being regularly presented with marvels of sexy buff Chris's on a regular basis.

And yes, I've decided that the collective noun for sexy Chris's is a "marvel," for obvious reasons.

So yes, it's arguably easier for men to be aroused by a sexy appearance. But does that mean they can be provoked beyond self-control?

Not exactly, no. Sexual arousal may be a powerful thing, but the brain also has many processes that counter it. The orbitofrontal cortex, for example, is implicated in regulating/suppressing sexual behaviour. One of the more sophisticated neurological regions, it's the part that says "this isn't a good idea, don't do it" when you're aroused or excited by an opportunity, particularly a sexual one, which won't have great long-term consequences.

The amygdala, mentioned earlier, also seems to play a role in determining appropriateness of arousal in context. Beautiful naked person standing before you in your bedroom? Sure, be aroused. Beautiful naked person standing before you in the supermarket, clutching a large knife? "Sexy fun time" is the wrong response here. And it's the amygdala that's believed to work this out.

However, it's possible for these restraining systems to be compromised. Alcohol can hinder the higher, complex areas like the orbitofrontal cortex while leaving the more primitive urges governing arousal intact. And the amygdala does what it can, but can only work with the information available. If the situation is ambiguous, or uncertain, it may make the wrong call.

Does this mean that men who sexually harass/assault women for what they're wearing are innocent after all?

No, of course not. A woman may choose to wear an alluring outfit, but it's still the man's choice to grope her without permission or invitation. If he's too drunk to hold back, it was his choice to get that drunk. "I couldn't help myself" is never an acceptable excuse for things like drink driving, and the same is true here. At least, it should be. "I'm responsible for my actions … except in this one particular scenario" is a feeble argument any way you slice it.

And if the social situation/context is a key part of determining whether sexual acts are acceptable, perhaps the fault lies with whoever creates and encourages scenarios where women can be manhandled with impunity, regardless of where you are or who you're with. Say, a gala dinner where the guests are all wealthy powerful men used to getting whatever they want, and the women are all young and vulnerable and not allowed to complain.

You could potentially pin the blame at many people when it comes to sexual assault, but it takes some warping of logic to pin it all on the women victims and their choice of outfits. But then, blaming the victims, usually the weakest and least powerful in any scenario, is a depressingly common human reaction, as it avoids tackling the bigger issues and challenging the status quo. Those who do it just can't seem to help themselves. Perhaps it's no wonder they often try to defend others who seem guilty of the same?

10

Nonconsensual Sex Has Taken On New Life in the Social Media Age

Kelly Oliver

Kelly Oliver is W. Alton Jones Professor of Philosophy at Vanderbilt University. She is the author of over 100 articles, 13 books, and 10 edited volumes. Her authored books include, most recently, Hunting Girls: Sexual Violence from *The Hunger Games* to Campus Rape *and* Earth and World: Philosophy After the Apollo Missions.

Lack of consent is valorized within popular culture to the point that sexual assault has become a spectator sport and creepshot entertainment on social media. Though it has a long and surprising history, new media has allowed the idea of bragging rights for nonconsensual sex to flourish. Indeed, as this viewpoint argues, the valorization of nonconsensual sex has reached the extreme where sex with unconscious girls, especially accompanied by photographs as trophies, has become a goal of some boys and men.

In an official trailer for the film *Pitch Perfect 2* (2015), Rebel Wilson's character "Fat Amy" is shown dancing at a campus party when the boy she is dancing with asks if she wants to have sex later. She says "no," but then gives him a suggestive wink. He looks confused and asks whether that means no or yes since she said "no," but then winked. She responds "absolutely not," and then

"Rape as Spectator Sport and Creepshot Entertainment: Social Media and the Valorization of Lack of Consent," by Kelly Oliver, *American Studies Journal*, Number 61 (2016), http://www.asjournal.org/61-2016/rape-spectator-sport-creepshot-entertainment-social-media-valorization-lack-consent/. Licensed under CC BY-SA 3.0.

winks again, suggesting that she doesn't mean what she said. What message does this send? When girls say "no," they really mean "yes"? Certainly, Amy's "no" is open for interpretation. In 2010 at Yale, fraternity brothers marched around the freshman dorms chanting, "No means yes, yes means anal" (Thomson-DeVeaux). Their interpretation of "no" and "yes" is clear.

The Yale case is not an isolated incident. Consider a chant used at St. Mary's University in Halifax to welcome new students: "SMU boys, we like them young. Y is for your sister, O is for oh so tight, U is for underage, N is for no consent, G is for grab that ass" (Williams 2013). A fraternity at Texas Tech was suspended for flying a banner that read "No Means Yes" (Schwarz). In 2013, another frat was suspended at Georgia Tech for distributing an email with the subject line "Luring your rapebait," which ended, "I want to see everyone succeed at the next couple parties" (Schwarz). And, in 2014 at William and Mary College, fraternity members sent around an email message, "never mind the extremities that surround it, the 99% of horrendously illogical bullshit that makes up the modern woman, consider only the 1%, the snatch" (McCarthy). The list goes on.

These examples suggest an aggressive campaign on the part of some fraternities to insist "No" means "Yes," meaning consent is not only irrelevant, but also undesired. In the St. Mary's chant, the lack of consent is openly valued, "N is for no consent." Actively seeking sex without consent, sometimes even admitting it is rape, turns them on. Whatever their actual desires, these college men are saying that they want nonconsensual sex. In fraternity culture, it seems their manhood and masculinity is dependent upon at least saying—or chanting—that they want forced sex, or sex with unconscious girls, if not also acting on it.[1] As we will see, sex with unconscious girls has become valorized in fraternity culture. Indeed, the valorization of nonconsensual sex has reached the extreme where sex with unconscious girls, especially accompanied by photographs as trophies, has become a goal of some college men.

In this essay, I argue that lack of consent is valorized within popular culture to the point that sexual assault has become a spectator sport and creepshot entertainment on social media. I trace this valorization of lack of consent back to the 14th Century Sleeping Beauty myth, on the one hand, and link it to pornographic fantasies of necrophilia and rape, on the other. I discuss the specific harms of "party rape" to sexual assault victims who are unconscious at the time and discover the violation of their bodies through photographs on social media. Finally, I consider how recording rather than reporting may become a new standard for prosecuting rape cases. Although rape and the valorization of it are not new, as we will see, the valorization of lack of consent is more public than ever. What used to be chanted in fraternity basements has taken to college quads. Furthermore, social media has simultaneously made rape and assault more visible and made it a form of social entertainment.

Pornography, Rape, and the Debasement of Women

Several studies have shown that many sexual predators buy into the pornographic fantasy that women enjoy being raped, what Nancy Bauer calls the "pornutopia" where everyone gets sexual satisfaction, even in rape (Bauer). One study concludes, "rapists, or men identified as unusually likely to rape, are characterized by the belief that rape is not averse to women—that, in fact, women desire and enjoy it" (Hamilton and Yee 112). Interviews with convicted rapists, and clinical reports indicate that many rapists "perceive their victims as deriving pleasure from the assault" (Hamilton and Yee 112).[2] Young men's attitudes towards consent are formed by exposure to pornography, especially easily accessed Internet porn, in which rape victims are depicted as enjoying sexual assault (see Cuthbertson 2015). In the world of pornography, the desires of the aggressor turns out to be the secret desires of the victim, whether or not she originally says "no." Of course, within the pornutopia, the agents are men who force their desires on women; and the fantasy is that women enjoy it, that "no" really does mean "yes, yes, yes."

This is the generous interpretation of the "No Means Yes" campaign on college campuses, namely, that these college men really believe that girls and women want to be raped. Perhaps fraternity brothers or college athletes who are prone to sexual assault have bought into the pornutopia, and at some level really believe that "No" mean "Yes." They have watched enough pornography to be convinced by the fantasy that whatever a woman says, and whether or not she is conscious, she enjoys it. The progression from aggressively trying to pressure girls and women to have sex, to using drugs and alcohol to weaken their defenses, has become the extreme of rendering them unconscious in order to sexually assault them, not only without their consent, but also at times, without their knowledge. For, within the pornutopia, the fantasy is that women enjoy violent sex, even abuse, conscious or not. If it turns him on, then within the logic of the pornutopia it turns her on too. This pornutopic fantasy of mutual satisfaction becomes a justification for acting on their violent desires.

The less generous interpretation is that they get off on debasing women, especially through rape. Slogans such as "no means yes," and "N is for no consent," suggest that rape and forced sex are desirable because they are debasing. Some studies show that men who rape women are more likely to have hostile attitudes towards women. The same is true for men who have nonconsensual sex with women. Researchers have found a strong correlation between negative attitudes and disrespect towards women and the proclivity for sexual assault (Lisak & Miller, Edwards et. al.). One study concludes, in terms of attitudes towards women, college men who say they would rape a woman if they could get away with it, and those who say they would force a woman to have intercourse, but don't call it rape, were distinguished only by levels of hostility and disrespect (Edwards et.al. 188). Whether college men who force nonconsensual sex buy into the pornutopic fantasy that women enjoy sexual assault whether they are conscious or unconscious, or they enjoy abusing women, it is clear that these college men valorize nonconsensual sex.

Recent cases of "creepshots" (photographs of girls and women taken and distributed without their consent or knowledge) found on fraternity websites, for example at Penn State, confirm the conclusion that men who prey on women sexually also enjoy debasing them. For, along with photographs of women in extremely compromising sexual positions, these websites include derogatory comments about the women by fraternity members. Or, consider media reports of videos taken by perpetrators in the high profile Vanderbilt rape case, which suggest that the college athletes who sexually assaulted an unconscious woman in a dorm room made derogatory remarks and jokes while engaging in the abuse. The same is true of the Steubenville, Ohio case where high school football players assaulted an unconscious girl while bystanders joked and made disparaging remarks about her. In this case, and others, perpetrators and/or by-standers have reportedly also peed on the unconscious victims, which suggests further denigration of these girls' and women's bodies.

The Fantasy of the Dead Girl and Sleeping Beauty

What are we to make of this desire to rape an unconscious "dead" girl? The fantasy of sex with an unconscious girl is centuries old, mythical even, with its first recorded roots in an anonymous 14th-century Catalan poem entitled "Frayre de Joy e Sor de Plaser" (Léglu 102). In this version of the Sleeping Beauty fairytale, after the beautiful virgin daughter of the emperor dies suddenly, her parents place her in a tower accessible by a bridge of glass. When Prince Frayre de Joy sees the sleeping beauty's smiling face, he "has sex repeatedly with the corpse" and gets her pregnant. The young prince attributes consent to the princess by kissing her a hundred times until her lips move in response (Léglu 106–7). As the legend of Sleeping Beauty shows, consent can become a male projection into his victim, whom he imagines as a properly active sexual partner, whereby he hallucinates consent, even pleasure. Sleeping Beauty may be a fairytale, but fairytales tell us something important about our cultural imaginary. The 14th-century tale of the rape of Sleeping Beauty, construed as mutually consenting sexual pleasure, is all too relevant to contemporary scenes of party rape of unconscious girls and women, and rape pornography. In term of attitudes toward rape, in some ways, we are still in the Middle Ages.

Newsweek magazine reports, "nearly one-third of college men admit they might rape a woman if they could get away with it" (qtd. in. Bekiempis). The results of the study, which found that approximately 32 percent of college men said they would force a woman to have sex, but only 13 percent of those said they would rape a woman (Edwards et. al.). This demonstrates the power of the word "rape." It also shows that the majority of men who would force a woman to have sex don't consider it rape. Indeed, if recent revelations brought to light via social media photos and videos are any indication, groups of young people happily watch, and even record, unconscious women being sexually assaulted without intervening or calling police. In another study, half of college men admit to using aggressive tactics to have sex (Wolitzky-Taylor et. al. 582).

As one study concludes, "college campuses foster date rape cultures, which are environments that support beliefs conducive to rape and increase risk factors related to sexual violence" (Burnett et. al.; see also Sanday). The existence of rape myths such as "victims are responsible for their own rapes," "victims are sluts and are asking for it," or "no" really means "yes," are prevalent on college campuses and part of the culture of fraternities and sports cultures. Although colleges and universities are institutions of higher learning, producing the most educated people in the country, they also breed rape myths at a higher rate than other cultural institutions. "Although rape myths are a social and cultural phenomenon that exists beyond the college campus, research suggests that athletics and fraternal organizations, replete on college campuses, are related to stronger rape-supportive attitudes" (Burnett et. al.; see also Bleecker & Murnen; Sanday). College athletics and fraternity culture perpetuate a classic double standard whereby men who have sex, even force sex, are "studs," whereas women who have sex are sluts (Burnett, Adams-Curtis & Forbes). In addition, several studies indicate that aggressive sports are correlated with aggressive sex: "College men who play aggressive sports in high school are more likely to accept rape myths, are more accepting of violence, and engage in more sexual coercion toward dating partners compared to other college men" (Forbes et. al., Burnett). The combination of a party atmosphere with alcohol flowing, and the acceptance of rape myths that include victim blaming or fantasies that victims enjoy rape makes colleges and universities especially fertile hunting grounds for serial rapists and men who are willing to force sex.

When highly educated men at Yale University can chant, "My name is Jack, I'm a necrophiliac. I f--k dead girls," and do so in public, we have to wonder if feminists have made any progress in addressing sexism (Thomson-DeVeaux). If in the past young men harbored such fantasies, they usually hid them. Now, claiming to sexually assault and rape, and imagining unconscious girls as "dead girls," are not only acceptable behaviors among young men, but also perhaps prerequisites to establish certain types of macho masculinity (see Buchwald). Obviously, these college men do not value consent. Indeed, sexual predators, including those involved in fraternity rape conspiracies value lack of consent. They aim for "nonconsensual sex," particularly through the use of drugs and alcohol to incapacitate their prey.

Specific Harms of Rape While Unconscious

Recent cases make vivid the corpse-like nature of unconscious "dead" girls who are sexually assaulted and raped. Girls who are unconscious when raped and then learn about their rape later through photographs, are literally forced to see their rape through the eyes of their rapists and the by-standers who saw it as a "Facebook" moment. They are forced to see their bodies as living corpses through the eyes of witnesses who claim they look "dead" and "lifeless."[3] Louise du Toit's discussion of the rape victim's experience of her own body as a "living corpse" takes on a new and powerful meaning in light of creepshots and videos recordings of sexual assaults. Victims view their own lifeless bodies being dragged, dropped, violated, abused, and raped, not as participants in the scene but as observers of it. Viewing their bodies as having undergone abuses that they don't remember, intensifies the damage to the victims' sense of their own identity and the coherence of their experience, further alienating them from their own experience and their own bodies. It works to undermine their confidence in their own ability to know themselves.[4]

Louise du Toit claims the damage rape does to victims is to make them see their own bodies through the eyes of their rapists as passive objects, and to see their own agency through the eyes of their rapists as powerless. The victim is treated like a thing. For the rapist her body has the advantages of a "corpse"—it can be used and abused with abandon—without the disadvantages, its abjection or putrification (du Toit 82). The victim is forced to confront her own mortality and her body as corpse. It splits her experience into seeing her body as a corpse while experiencing it as a living body; she becomes a sort of living corpse. Of course, du Toit is speaking metaphorically when she talks of the corpse-like feeling of victims who were conscious of their attacks. She is not talking about recent cases of unconscious girls whose limp bodies were dragged around, violated, and described as "dead girls" completely "lifeless," a "living corpse." For girls and women who are victims of nonconsensual sex, sexual assault, or rape while unconscious, referred to as "dead girls" by their rapists, and later shown pictures of their own inanimate bodies being violated, the perception of their bodies as a living corpse is even more dramatic.

Discovering that one has been raped while unconscious can cause different types and levels of harm than the trauma of sexual assault while awake.[5] The fact that victims discover their victimization from third parties or recordings undermines a sense of coherent existence that cuts to the heart of the sense of self. It is as if this happened to someone else and yet undeniably did not.

The victim may come to question herself, to experience her life as fragmented, and to fear unconsciousness, even sleep. As Cressida Heyes argues, "women who have been sexually assaulted while unconscious report that they become hyper-vigilant, unable to close their eyes for fear of losing control and becoming vulnerable again" (Heyes). Rape while unconscious damages the victim's sense of herself as an agent in ways unique to this form of rape. Victims who are raped while unconscious or asleep may find restful sleep impossible, fearing that if they go to sleep or pass out, they will be attacked again. Furthermore, they can no longer rely on the "anonymity of sleep," a time when every living creature requires a safe space to retreat from the world (Heyes). The anonymity of sleep is further disturbed if images of the victim's sleeping body are disseminated through social media. What should be a time of restful recovery and restoration becomes a dangerous time of special vulnerability to sexual assault followed by ridicule through social media.

Social Media and Continued Victimization

Perpetrators can continue their victimization of targets of sexual assault using social media. Posting photographs and jeering comments extends the damage to victims beyond the rape itself. "Sexual assault is a crime of power and dominance," says psychologist Rebecca Campbell. "By distributing images of the rape through social media, this is a way of asserting dominance and power to hurt the victim over and over again" (Fuchs et. al.). Rape has become a spectator sport in which rapists pose for the camera and victims are subject to creepshots distributed or posted as trophies or entertainment, which adds a new layer of trauma and shame onto these crimes. Photographs and videos have been used to further torment and shame victims, adding another layer of victimization to the sexual assault itself (Shim). The trauma of victimization not only becomes public, but also infinitely repeatable. It can go viral. It doesn't go away. Its presence on social media extends the victimization and trauma into an infinite future that makes closure or healing more difficult, if not impossible (Heyes).

Indeed, the shame over photographs of their naked bodies in compromising positions being treated as living corpses has led some victims to kill themselves rather than face public scorn. For example, in April 2013, in two distinct cases, teenage girls killed themselves after photographs of their sexual assaults were posted online (Fuchs). In text messages, they both suggested that they couldn't go on living with the public shame of everyone seeing their violated bodies. Many rape survivors feel shame over being sexually assaulted, even when they don't blame themselves, and even when only their perpetrator knows about it. Social media and the public spectacle of party rape intensifies this shame, and adds another layer of shame, namely the shame of being photographed while compromised and victimized. The dissemination of creepshot photographs of sexual assault adds another type of trauma to the trauma of sexual assault. Friends and strangers, anyone with access to the Internet, might see pictures that compound the trauma of sexual assault and take its harms to another level.

Many feminists have discussed the devastating effects of rape on victims.[6] For example, du Toit claims that the victim's world is "unmade" (du Toit). Discussing her own rape, Susan Brison says, "I felt as if I was experiencing things posthumously," which resonates with the idea of one's own body as a living corpse (Brison 8). Brison and du Toit discuss this living corpse-like experience for rape victims who are aware of their rapes, relive them, testify to them, and continue to be traumatized by the experience of them afterwards. But for a woman who sees her rape for the first time through the eyes of others, this experience of one's own body as not one's own, as one's own body as a living corpse, can only be intensified. And for women whose sexual assault is documented, recorded, and posted on social media, the reliving of the incident and the retraumatization is extended indefinitely.

Ann Cahill argues, "rape, in its total denial of the victim's agency, will, and personhood, can be understood as a denial of intersubjectivity itself" (Cahill 132). Certainly, rendering their victims unconscious is an effective way for rapists to avoid dealing with the intersubjectivity usually involved in having sex, consensual or nonconsensual. Sexual predators deny intersubjectivity by using rape drugs and alcohol to insure that their victims are not conscious or only semiconscious. This strategy not only makes it easier to rape girls and women, but also allows the perpetrator to avoid the intersubjective dimension of sex. In these scenarios, girls and women function as "living dolls" with which men pleasure themselves. Drugs and alcohol can leech the victim's subjectivity from the scene and make her more like an object or "living corpse" than a sex partner, or even a resisting victim. They may also leech the rapist's sense of guilt or responsibility, helping him absolve himself of the crime by saying, "what she doesn't know won't hurt her." Or, as one participant claimed in the Steubenville, Ohio rape case, "we don't know whether or not she wanted it." Like the rapist prince in the legend of Sleeping Beauty, these perpetrators may even imagine that their victims enjoyed it.

Open Valorization of Lack of Consent

The growing use of rape drugs and alcohol to render girls unconscious, and thereby easily rapeable, combined with sentiments expressed in the Yale fraternity chant, "My name is Jack, I'm a necrophiliac, I f--k dead girls," suggest a valorization and eroticiziation of sex with unconscious girls. Consider, for example, in 2014, a fraternity at the University of Wisconsin planned a party to incapacitate "hot" girls using punch spiked with the drug Rohypnol (flunitrazepam); the girls were given an all-you-can-drink pass, and their hands were marked with a red-X, presumably so that fraternity brothers could easily make out their targets.[7] Several girls ended up in the hospital. Rape drugs can be lethal at high doses. It is unclear whether or not the "rape conspiracy" was successful at the University of Wisconsin. If the girls were drugged unconscious and had no memory of sexual assault, how would we know, unless the perpetrators confessed or the hospitals used rape-kits? Using drugs like Rohypnol help insure that the victim can't testify against her rapist, especially if she remains unconscious during the entire attack. What is clear is that in cases involving date-rape drugs, the goal on the part of perpetrators is to incapacitate their victims and make them easy prey for sexual assault. The goal is to have sex with a passive, unconscious, unresponsive, "lifeless" girl. Lack of consent is assumed. Nonconsensual sex with an unconscious woman puts the man in complete control of the woman's body. Certainly, "sex" with inanimate girls is not about intimacy, and perhaps not even pleasure, but control. These fraternity men are trophy hunting for prime party rape prey. As the Yale chant suggests, these fraternity men want sex with "dead girls."

Perhaps this valorization and eroticization of sex with "dead girls," a form of pseudo-necrophilia, is also a product of pornography, especially zombie porn or snuff porn. If intelligent college students want to have sex with unconscious girls, this form of pseudo-necrophilia as the ultimate macho sexual power trip has become eroticized in our culture. Of course, social media is filled with pornographic images of naked women, whether it is professionally made porn, pornographic selfies, or creepshots. Pornography has penetrated mainstream culture, not just with the prevalence and availability of pornography on the Internet, but also in our everyday lives (Green, Bauer 77–78). The "mainstream penetration" of pornography is evident in "the way people are presenting themselves for cameras," which "is much more sexualized than it once was" (Green). Pornographic photographs have also become part of party rape. Creepshots of party rape are circulated on social media. It is noteworthy that in most of the recent high profile rape cases there have been groups of young men involved, some of whom took photos and videos using cellphones. This suggests that rape has become a spectator sport worthy of candid photographs to be disseminated during and after the event. These young men are "having fun," and they see the photographs of naked "dead" girls in compromising positions as "funny."[8] Pseudo-necrophilia has gone mainstream.

Has absolute powerlessness on the part of girls and women become the height of a new erotic fantasy? Has this form of pseudo-necrophilia become a new norm for sex on college campuses? Recent cases of sexual assault on unconscious "dead" girls suggest that something about the victim's complete powerlessness and lack of agency has become erotic, fun, or even funny. In addition to the eroticization of unconscious women, then, it is crucial to consider the power dynamics in sexually violating someone powerless to resist. Raping an unconscious woman is the ultimate power trip, proving absolute dominance over another human being, and a woman in particular. And pictures of sexual assault have become new forms of trophies mounted on the Internet.

As I pointed out earlier, some scholars have argued that sports culture, military culture, and other aspects of dominant culture, including movies and video games, promote the idea that masculinity is gained and proved by dominating girls and women, especially through sex and rape.[9] Although rape and the connection to masculinity is not new, it is particularly troubling that rape is becoming openly valorized, as evidenced by groups of college men chanting rape slogans, and the value put on lack of consent also endorsed in these slogans. Rape is becoming a group activity with spectators. And, in some cases, it is a planned event, as for example, in the fraternities accused of "rape conspiracy" for serving punch spiked with rape drugs in order to incapacitate their "rapebait" (Swartz, Frampton). While there always has been rape, including gang rape, what seems new is the public valorization of "nonconsensual sex" and its display on social media. If in the past rapists acted in the shadows and kept their acts a secret, now they chant in public about rape, record their sexual assaults, and post pictures for entertainment online. Rape has become a form of public entertainment.

Recording, Not Reporting: "Pictures Don't Lie (Women Do)"

Ironically, in some recent high profile cases, because the victims were unconscious—and in some cases didn't even know they had been raped—rape was easier to prove, try, and convict. This suggests that the "testimony" of unconscious girls is more believable than that of conscious ones. While the testimony of young women is challenged, discounted, and often at best put into the context of He-Said versus She-Said, the recent phenomenon of creepshot photographs of rapes, and recording of unconscious rape victims taken with cell phone cameras, has brought about some high-profile convictions. As one detective said in the Vanderbilt rape case, "pictures don't lie" ("Steubenville"). In spite of statistics that false reporting is extremely low, too often the suspicion is that rape victims can and do lie.[10] In some recent high profile cases, however, the victim didn't even know she had been raped. In these cases, the rape was recorded and not reported. And, in these cases, it seems that the mute "testimony" of a visually "lifeless" "dead girl" is more powerful than the sorrowful testimony of victims aware of their attacks.

For example, on June 23rd 2013, an unconscious Vanderbilt honors student was gang raped by four Vanderbilt football players, two of whom were later convicted on all counts, and two of whom have yet to stand trial, as of this writing.[11] The victim has no memory of the rapes. The next day, her then boyfriend and one of the perpetrators, Brandon Vandenburg, reportedly told her that she'd vomited in his room and he'd taken care of her all night. Embarrassed, she thanked him. Two days later, investigating vandalism in the dorm, campus police saw surveillance videos of the football players dragging the unconscious woman down the hallway of the dorm, taking her into Vandenburg's room, then going in and out of the dorm room, dragging the half-naked unconscious woman, dropping her several times, giggling, smiling, and happily taking pictures of her, even close ups of her butt, and at one point covering the surveillance camera with a towel.

Supposedly, Vandenburg's roommate was asleep on the top bunk during part of the assault and later left the room. Several other men in the dorm saw the football players manhandling the unconscious woman, several men saw the videos of the rape, even while it was going on, and not one of them reported it to authorities. Two of Vandenburg's friends in California received photos and videos throughout the night, one of them commenting in a message back to Vandenburg that they should "gang bang" the "bitch," make sure she "doesn't wake up," and then "get rid of her." (WKRN Staff)

By the end of the investigation, police had confiscated cellphone photographs and videos of rape, sodomy with a water bottle, and other acts of sexual assault. In their own words, the players were "clowning" for the camera. They were taking pictures as if they were on vacation, to show their sexual prowess, and because they thought it was funny. At first, the victim denied that she'd been raped. She couldn't believe it. The police had to show her the photographs and videos in order to prove it to her. When interviewed, the detectives said this was the first time that they had to convince the victim that she'd been raped. Rather than being reported, the rape was recorded.

As strange as it seems, recording instead of reporting is becoming more common. Girls are finding out they've been raped when pictures taken by the rapists or by-standers are posted on social media or sent around as text messages. For example, on August 11th, 2012, in Steubenville, Ohio an unconscious high school student was sexually assaulted while by-standers watched. Photographs and videos that circulated on social media showed the perpetrators talking about rape while assaulting her. Later, texts and tweets also joked about rape, making light of the fact that the girl was "so raped," and slept through "a wang in the butthole" (Ley). The victim didn't know that she'd been raped until she saw the pictures. The boy who posted photographs was found guilty of distributing child pornography since the girl was under age (Davidson). And, one of the perpetrators defended himself, saying, "It isn't really rape because you don't know if she wanted to or not" (Ley). This sentiment makes clear that in these young people's minds, or at least in this person's mind, consent and desire are not only mental states, but also the same mental state.[12] Furthermore, the fantasy is that if a girl is unconscious, and neither affirmative nor negative consent can be given, "sex" with her is not really rape. Echoing the age-old myth of Sleeping Beauty, these men imagined their unconscious victim actually might be consenting, perhaps even "wanting" it.

Many rape cases that come to light via social media or cellphone photographs feature groups of people, mostly men, watching as unconscious girls are dragged, dropped, sexually abused, and photographed. Some of these by-standers take pictures with their phones rather than report the crimes. In these cases, cellphones become part of the sexual assault. Rapists and by-standers take pictures for fun or entertainment, and generally to enhance the experience. They have even more "fun" distributing the pictures to friends or on social media sites. Take, for example, a young woman who first discovered she had been gang raped on Panama City beach in Florida when a video appeared on the nightly news. Hundreds of people watched. Seemingly part of the scenery or entertainment on that crowded beach, someone recorded it using a cell phone (Stapleton). Reportedly, she was drugged with a drink offered to her on the beach and then two Troy University (Alabama) students sexually assaulted her. A spokesperson for the local sheriff's office said, "there's a number of videos we've recovered with things similar to this, and I can only imagine how many things we haven't recovered." Through social media "we have been able to find video of girls, incoherent and passed out, and almost like they are drugged, being assaulted on the beaches of Panama City in front of a bunch of people standing around" watching (Stapleton). A popular Spring Break destination for college students, Florida beaches are also a hotspot for college rapists who prey on intoxicated girls. Perhaps as troubling as the sexual assault itself is the fact that rather than help the victims, by-standers watch or take videos and post them online.

Pictures of unconscious girls in compromising positions are sent around like funny cat videos. While these images retraumatize the victim and celebrate sexual violation; they can also be used as hard evidence of sexual assault or rape, which, as we've seen, is notoriously difficult to prove, and even more difficult to prosecute and convict (Carmon). Pictures and videos taken as part of the "fun" of sexual assault can be used to convince a jury that assault took place (Grinberg). They also are making it apparent to our culture at large that sexual violence is considered "fun" and "funny" by lots of young people who enjoy a good party, especially if it involves unconscious girls (Shim). But, as we've seen, for victims, their humiliation can go viral and seemingly last forever on social media (Shim). As noted earlier, two rape victims killed themselves in response to social media pictures of, and comments about, their rapes while unconscious (Shim). College student Elisa Lopez was sexually assaulted on the subway and subsequently traumatized by a creepshot video circulating on the Internet. She said that she could recover from the attack, but the video wouldn't go away. The video haunted her and made it impossible for her to continue with her life as she had before (Filipovic). This is the case with many of the victims whose sexual assault is circulated or posted on social media. Many of them find the public humiliation even more traumatic and upsetting than the sexual assault itself.

In addition to becoming part of the harassment of victims, photographs taken by the perpetrators also can be used against them in court. New apps for cellphones, however, such as Snapchat where pictures or messages sent around disappear after twenty-four hours, or YikYak where messages disappear, seem designed to circumvent this possibility. But, even these apps are bringing to light rapes and victimization that may have remained hidden otherwise. For example, YikYak chatting at Stanford revealed that an eighteen-year-old girl, who was unconscious at the time, was raped by a Stanford varsity swimmer, described as "a clean-cut star athlete" and "the all-American boy next door" (Glenza & Carroll). Rumors about the sexual assault circulating on YikYak eventually

[led] to an investigation into a crime that might otherwise never have been reported. Social media, then, can serve a complicated double function when it comes to sexual assault and rape. On the one hand, it can be used to further humiliate and harass victims of sexual assault. On the other hand, it can be used to alert authorities to sex crimes and it can provide evidence to try and convict perpetrators.

Social Media and the Objectification of Women

Arguably, social media such as Facebook, Snapchat, and Tinder were invented as part of a culture that objectifies and denigrates girls and women. It is well known that Facebook founder and Harvard graduate Mark Zuckerberg, now one of the richest men in the country, invented the social media site Facebook to post pictures of girls for his college buddies to rate and berate (Egan). And, it was recently uncovered that Stanford graduate Evan Spiegel, inventor of Snapchat, which is estimated to be worth at least three billion dollars, sent messages during his days in a fraternity referring to women as "bitches," "sororisluts," to be "peed on," and discussed getting girls drunk to have sex with them (Hu). The wildly popular hook-up site Tinder, with 1.6 billion "swipes" and 26 million matches a day, has changed the way people date (Yi). Now using proximity sensors, the mobile app allows users to view pictures and swipe right if they like what they see and swipe left if not. If there is a match between two users who swipe right, then they can message each other or "keep playing." Tinder was seeded on college campuses by former University of California students and co-founders Sean Rad and Justin Mateen; it has generated new urban slang, "tinderslut" to refer to women who use Tinder to hook-up with men. Rad and Mateen faced criticism when they gave the term two emojie thumbs up on social media.

Both Tinder co-founders are also involved in a sexual harassment suit wherein Mateen is accused of severely and repeatedly harassing the former vice president of marketing for Tinder, Whitney Wolfe, who claims that he sent her harassing sexist messages calling her a "slut," a "gold-digger," and a "whore," along with insulting her in public while Rad watched on and did nothing (Bercovici). Wolfe also claims that Rad and Mateen refused to name her as a co-founder because she is "a girl" (Bercovici). Given the continued use of social media to target, harass, and humiliate young women, it is telling that all of these technologies were born out of sexist attitudes towards women. Facebook and Snapchat were explicitly designed to denigrate women. And, many social media sites, like other forms of traditional media, bank on images of attractive girls and women. Photographs of girls and women looking sexy and cute are the mainstay of some sites, especially creepshot sites.

"Creepshots," as they are called, are photographs of women's bodies taken without their consent. The lack of consent is essential, as is outlined on websites that specialize in creepshots such as Tumblr's creepshooter, creepshots.com, and metareddit's creepshots. Metareddit's website specifies, "Creepshots are CANDID. If a person is posting for and/or aware that a picture is being taken, then it is no longer candid and ceases to be a creepshot. A creepshot captures the natural, raw sexiness of the subject ... Use stealth, cunning and deviousness to capture the beauty of your unsuspecting, chosen target." Clearly, girls and women are seen as unsuspecting "targets," prey to be "shot" and "captured" on film. They are cut into pieces, valued for the body parts, anonymously taken from them by the camera and posted online. On all of these creepshot websites, there are subcategories such as "ass," "poop sex," "crouch," "boobs," "jailbait," and "teen."[13]

Some creepshot videos end up on pornographic sites. For example, college student Elisa Lopez was in disbelief when a coworker showed her a video circulating online in which a man was penetrating her with his fingers as she lay passed out on the subway train after partying with friends. Rather than help her, some by-stander took a video and posted it online. Lopez tried without success to get the video taken down. Traumatized by the video, even more than the sexual assault, Lopez became depressed, her schoolwork suffered, and she almost ended up in the mental ward of the hospital. Although getting better, years afterwards, Lopez is still traumatized by the creepshot video (Filipovic). Because of the vigilance of Lopez and her friends, eventually a suspect was arrested for the sexual assault, but not for the creepshot, which damaged Lopez as much, if not more, than the assault itself (Dow).

Creepshots are valued because of the lack of consent on the part of the subject. Her agency is described as "vain attempts at putting on a show for the camera," and thus to be evacuated from the images.[14] Creepshooters are likened to hunters choosing a target. The camera is their weapon. Subjects of creepshots do not give their consent. Indeed, insofar as women are unaware that they are being photographed, they cannot give consent, unless moving through the world in their everyday activities wearing their everyday clothes (see "yoga pants" as a subcategory of creepshots) constitutes consent. This suggests that women's bodies are public property; or that when women are in public, they are fair game, especially if they are wearing creepshot-worthy clothes. Creepshots display not only the "sexy" girl or her body part, but also the hunting prowess of the creeper photographer. This suggests a disturbing analogy to the rape of unconscious girls, especially now that creepshots are increasingly becoming part of the violation. Their lack of consent is the conquest, documented now through creepshot photographs posted online as trophies. Within this world of creepshots and rape drugs, nonconsensual sex is valued because the lack of consent is considered "hot."

As became apparent in both the Steubenville and Vanderbilt cases, along with the sexual assaults, taking creepshot photographs of unconscious naked girls or women and distributing them is a crime. In both cases, perpetrators were found guilty not only of rape, but also of taking and distributing illegal photographs. In the Steubenville case, perpetrators were charged with distributing child pornography (the victim was only sixteen). In the Vanderbilt case, Brandon Vandenburg's lawyer claimed "all" he was guilty of was taking the photos, and explained the cover-up saying, "at least he had the good sense to be upset afterwards" (Warren and Spargo). What also became apparent in these cases is the photographs and videos were an important part of the rape itself. The college men smiled and clowned for the camera, joked and jeered for posterity, and took pleasure not only in sexually abusing their victims, but also in capturing it on film, and then sharing it with friends. Reportedly, in the Vanderbilt case, Corey Batey told Brandon Vandenburg to "get this on camera," as he raped their unconscious victim.

In sum, while rape and debasement of women are not new, the use of social media to do so is. The use of ubiquitous cellphone cameras to take creepshots of unsuspecting women, including unconscious rape victims, makes clear that contemporary mainstream youth culture values lack of consent. In other words, it is not just that some men will take pictures or have sex without a woman's consent, but also photographs are valued more where there is no consent. Moreover, with creepshots, by definition the lack of consent must be obvious. The photograph needs to display the unsuspecting woman or her body parts, along with the fact that she doesn't know that she's being photographed. Of course, this makes an unconscious woman the perfect subject for creepshots. In addition, seeing women in compromising positions, naked, or sexually violated, is considered "funny." Again, candid camera or humor in humiliating photos has been around since photography itself, and so has pornography. If men used to secretly share pictures of naked women, however, now they do so publicly. And whereas in the past, pornographic pictures were produced for mass consumption but sold privately, even wrapped in brown paper and only to adults, now the Internet is filled with selfie porn, sexting photos, and creepshots of women who are not professionals. Rapists hamming for the camera, and taking creepshots of unsuspecting unconscious girls, are part and parcel of the patriarchal pornutopia in the age of social media.

Notes

1. For a discussion of the relationship between rape and manhood and masculinity, see Kimmel and Miedzian in *Transforming a Rape Culture*. In that same volume, Michael Messner discusses the relationship between violence towards women and sports culture.
2. See studies by Tieger, Malamuth & Check, Scully & Marolla, Clark & Lewis, and Gager & Schurr.
3. This is the way bystanders and the rapists described the victim of the Steubenville, Ohio rape and the way the juror described the video of the Vanderbilt rape victim.
4. For an insightful phenomenology of the effects of rape while unconscious or semi-conscious see Heyes. The author analyzes the importance of the anonymity and vulnerability of sleep, which becomes impossible for women raped while asleep.
5. US Department of Education, Office for Civil Rights, "Dear Colleague Letter: Sexual Violence, Background, Summary, and Fast Facts," 4 Apr. 2011, 2ed.gov, web, 15 June 2015. For discussions of PTSD and trauma resulting from sexual assault, and from the reporting of sexual assault, see Ullman & Peter-Hagene, Au et al., and Leiner et. al. These studies show that PTSD and/or depression frequently occur in victims after sexual assault. Reactions to victim's reporting dramatically affects subsequent symptoms (Ullman & Peter-Hagene).
6. According to a government report, "Victims of sexual assault are more likely to suffer academically and from depression, post-traumatic stress disorder, to abuse alcohol and drugs, and to contemplate suicide." Suicide.org reports that 33 percent of rape victims contemplate suicide and 13 percent of rape victims will commit suicide (Caruso). See also Archard, Brison, and Kim.
7. "Many women who attended the party had the red X on their hands, leading authorities to believe that they were part of a color-coded and premeditated plan to target certain individuals for possible date rape" (Mejia).
8. News reports of the Steubenville rape of a high school teenager and reports of rape of a Vanderbilt Senior include remarks by men involved that make clear they considered their actions "clowning" around, or fun, and the pictures of the girls as funny (Dean, Lay).
9. See Bruni. See also Jones, Jensen, and Messerschmidt. Robert Jensen describes "dominant masculinity" as "ready to rape" and "numbed, disconnected, shut down" (Jensen 185). In a 2000 study, James Messerschmidt found that adolescent male sexual violence was often motivated by social pressures to prove their masculinity.
10. Certainly the case of "Jackie" who reported a terrible gang rape at the University of Virginia, covered by *The Rolling Stone*, which subsequently turned out to be false, didn't help the cause of rape victims (Erdely, Coronel et. al.).
11. In July 2015, Vandenburg and Batey's original trial was declared a mistrial because one of the jurors was once a party in a sexual assault case. A new trial is set for November 2015.
12. For a philosophical delineation of differences between consent and desire, see Schulhofer.
13. See http://metareddit.com/r/CreepShots/.
14. Ibid.

11

Why #MeToo Additions Need Time

Denise-Marie Ordway

Denise-Marie Ordway writes for Journalist's Resource, a database for journalists based at the Shorenstein Center on Media, Politics, and Public Policy at the Harvard Kennedy School. She has worked as a reporter for newspapers and radio stations in the United States and Central America, including the Orlando Sentinel *and* Philadelphia Inquirer. *Her work also has appeared in publications such as* USA TODAY, *the* New York Times, Chicago Tribune *and* Washington Post.

Many victims of sexual assault have either never come forward or waited years or even decades to point the finger of accusation against those they claim to be perpetrators. Some people have criticized women for letting so much time pass by, claiming that such delays cast doubt on accusations. In this viewpoint the author provides clear reasons, citing self-blame, fear, shame, and other factors, why victims may not report assaults right away. She offers several reasons why reporting attacks has been discouraged through research done on individual cases.

O ver the past year, as the #MeToo movement has grown and national figures such as Supreme Court Justice Brett Kavanaugh and movie mogul Harvey Weinstein have faced allegations of sexual misconduct from women they knew years ago, one question has continued to surface:

Why would someone claiming abuse wait so long to come forward?

Research indicates the answer is complicated. There are a wide range of reasons people don't report their experiences with sexual harassment and assault to authorities and, oftentimes, even hide them from friends and family members.

One reason is self-blame, said Karen G. Weiss, an associate professor of sociology at West Virginia University whose research focuses on sexual violence.

"The public may not realize just how many victims of any crime blame themselves for their own victimization," Weiss told Journalist's Resource in an e-mail interview. "Self-blame is often reified by 'well-intentioned' confidants to whom they disclose. Seemingly innocent questions from family and friends can trigger self-doubt and prevent victims from reporting to police. They may also question what they did wrong and believe it was their fault."

Another reason: Many people who have been raped don't recognize it as rape, even when it fits the legal definition, a finding revealed in a review of 28 academic studies.

Below, we've gathered and summarized a sampling of peer-reviewed research—including two academic articles from Weiss—that investigates why many people don't report sex crimes. This list includes studies that look at factors that discourage or prevent reporting among specific groups, including teenagers, college students, prison inmates and women serving in the military.

"Meta-Analysis of the Prevalence of Unacknowledged Rape"
Wilson, Laura C.; Miller, Katherine E.; *Trauma, Violence, & Abuse,* **April 2016.**

Laura C. Wilson, an assistant professor of psychology at the University of Mary Washington, led this review of 28 academic studies to estimate how often women who've been sexually assaulted do not label their experience as rape. The 28 studies focused on the experiences of a total of 5,917 women who had been raped at some point in their lives after age 14.

Across the studies, the researchers find that 60.4 percent of women, on average, did not recognize their experience as rape even though it fit the definition—an unwanted sexual experience obtained through force or the threat of force or a sexual experience they did not consent to because they were incapacitated.

"This finding has important implications because it suggests that our awareness of the scope of the problem may underestimate its true occurrence rate, depending on the type of measurement," the authors write. "This impacts policy reform, allocations of mental health services, survivors' perceptions of their experiences, and society's attitudes toward survivors."

The authors stress that their results may not generalize to men who have experienced sexual assault or to women who experienced it before age 14.

"'You Just Don't Report That Kind of Stuff': Investigating Teens' Ambivalence Toward Peer-Perpetrated, Unwanted Sexual Incidents"
Weiss, Karen G.; *Violence and Victims*, 2013.
In this study, Weiss investigates why many teenagers who experience unwanted sexual contact from other teens trivialize those experiences as unimportant or normal. She relies on data from the National Crime Victimization Survey, administered each year to tens of thousands of individuals aged 12 years and older. Weiss examined information collected on sex-related incidents between 1992 and 2000.

According to survey data, 92 percent of teens who say they experienced some form of unwanted sexual contact are girls, 81 percent are white and 13 percent are Hispanic. Just over half of these incidents—53 percent—involved sexual coercion such as rape and attempted rape while 47 percent involved other contact such as groping. Almost half of teenagers—44 percent—said the perpetrators were other youth between the ages of 12 and 17.

A key finding: Teens who experience unwanted contact rarely report it. Five percent of incidents were reported to police and 25 percent were reported to other authorities such as school officials or employers.

Weiss finds two common reasons why teenagers don't report perpetrators who are teenagers: 1) uncertainty that the incidents are real crimes or worth reporting and 2) adaptive indifference, which she describes as "an avoidance response that allows teens to do nothing, thereby remaining loyal to their friends, dating partners, schoolmates and peer groups."

"Ambiguity reflects the difficulties of recognizing crime due to cultural messages that trivialize certain situations (e.g., sexual coercion by dates and unwanted sexual contact by schoolmates) as normal or as an inevitable part of youth," Weiss writes. "Indifference reflects the social pressures for teens to 'do the right thing,' which often means conforming to group norms that discourage reporting to police. In this manner, ambivalence protects teens, at least temporarily, from social disapproval and interpersonal conflict associated with disclosing peer offenses."

"Too Ashamed to Report: Deconstructing the Shame of Sexual Victimization"
Weiss, Karen G.; *Feminist Criminology*, July 2010.
In another study from Weiss, she "deconstructs shame as both a culturally imbued response to sexual victimization and as a much taken-for-granted reason for why victims don't report incidents to the police."

Weiss analyzed statements made by men and women as part of the annual National Crime Victimization Survey. She examined their responses to a survey question asking them to describe what happened to them. She also examined structured responses to questions about sex-related incidents. The federal Bureau of Justice Statistics allowed her to access photocopies of information collected from survey respondents between 1992 and early 2000. The sample for this study consisted of 116 females and 20 males, most of whom were under age 25.

What Weiss found was that many respondents expressed shame as part of their description of what happened and why they didn't go to the police. Thirteen percent of incidents made some reference to shame. For example, a 19-year-old women stated that she was ashamed and felt partly to blame for a male acquaintance raping her because she couldn't stop him.

"Foremost, women's shame narratives draw upon cultural assumptions about how 'good girls' should behave and how 'bad girls' will be judged after rape or sexual assault," Weiss writes. "Women fearing they will be blamed, disgraced, or defamed are often too ashamed to report sexual victimization to the police."

Shame also was a strong deterrent for men.

"Acknowledging crimes that are not supposed to happen to men, or at least real men, may threaten their masculinity, and challenge their sexual identities," Weiss writes. "Unwilling to risk emasculation or exposure, men are choosing to remain silent rather than report sexual victimization to the police and others."

"Barriers to Reporting Sexual Assault for Women and Men: Perspectives of College Students"
Sable, Marjorie R.; Danis, Fran; Mauzy, Denise L.; Gallagher, Sarah K.; *Journal of American College Health,* **2006.**

For this study, a research team from the University of Missouri-Columbia surveyed students at a large, Midwestern university to better understand what they perceive as the biggest barriers to reporting rape and sexual assault for men and women. Of the 215 students who participated, 54.7 percent were female and 83.6 percent were white.

Students rated "shame, guilt and embarrassment," "confidentiality concerns" and "fear of not being believed" as the top three perceived barriers to reporting rape among both men and women. However, students rated shame, guilt and embarrassment as a much larger barrier for men than women. Another major barrier to reporting for men, according to students, is the fear they could be judged as being gay.

"Compared with women, men may fail to report because reporting is perceived to jeopardize their masculine self-identity," the authors write. "The high score that being judged as gay received by the respondents may acknowledge society's consideration that male rape occurs in the gay, not the general, community."

Among the barriers perceived to be much larger for women than for men were "lack of resources to obtain help," "cultural or language barriers to obtaining help" and "financial dependence on perpetrator/perpetrator interference in seeking help."

"Reporting Sexual Assault in the Military: Who Reports and Why Most Servicewomen Don't"

Mengeling, Michelle A.; Booth, Brenda M.; Torner, James C.; Sadler, Anne G.; *American Journal of Preventive Medicine*, **July 2014.**

For this study, researchers interviewed women who had served in the US Army or Air Force and acknowledged at least one attempted or completed sexual assault while they were in the military. Of the 1,339 women interviewed, 18 percent said they had experienced sexual assault while serving on full-time active duty. Meanwhile, 12 percent said they had experienced sexual assault while serving in the Reserves or National Guard.

Among the key findings: Three-fourths of servicewomen did not report their assaults. Eighty percent of women who said they'd been assaulted identified the perpetrator as US military personnel. The researchers found that sexual assaults were more likely to be reported if they occurred on base or while on duty or if they resulted in a physical injury. They also found that enlisted women who had never gone to college were most likely to report.

The most common reasons women gave for not officially reporting their assault were embarrassment and not knowing how to report. Other common reasons included worries about how reporting might affect their careers and whether confidentiality would be kept. Some women believed nothing would be done and some blamed themselves for their experiences. A few women said they did not report because the person they had to report to was the perpetrator or a friend of the perpetrator.

"Study results reinforce earlier work showing that servicewomen continue to significantly underreport SAIM [sexual assault in the military]," the authors write. "For many servicewomen, the disadvantages of reporting outweigh the advantages."

"The Darkest Figure of Crime: Perceptions of Reasons for Male Inmates to Not Report Sexual Assault"
Miller, Kristine Levan; *Justice Quarterly,* **2010.**

Kristine Levan, an assistant professor of sociology at the University of Idaho, surveyed a random sample of 890 inmates from eight state-run prisons in Texas to understand why a male prisoner might not report sexual assault. Because many inmates didn't complete the survey or completed it incorrectly, the final sample is 396 men.

Inmates said the three most common reasons prisoners may not report sexual assault are embarrassment, retaliation from other inmates and a fear of harassment and abuse from other inmates.

"The male prison environment thrives on exerting one's own masculinity," Levan writes. "Although the assailant of a sexual assault gains respect and status, the victim is ultimately emasculated … Heralding back to the tenets of the convict code, inmates are expected to not show signs of weakness, especially to other inmates, and admission to sexual victimization may be an indication to other inmates that they are indeed weak."

Another key finding: The reason for not reporting may differ according to an inmate's age.

"As the age of an inmate increases, he is more likely to report a fear of harassment, rather than embarrassment, as the primary reason to not report a sexual assault," the author writes. "The general consensus in the existing literature indicates that younger inmates are more likely to be sexually abused."

"Would They Officially Report an In-Prison Sexual Assault? An Examination of Inmate Perceptions"
Fowler, Shannon K.; Blackburn, Ashley G.; Marquart, James W.; Mullings, Janet L.; *The Prison Journal*, 2010.

A research team led by Shannon K. Fowler, an associate professor at the University of Houston, examines whether prisoners would report sexual violence or recommend that other prisoners report violence they had experienced. The team surveyed 935 male and female inmates from a large Southern prison system.

Here's what they found: Most inmates said they would report their sexual assault. However, those who already had experienced assault while incarcerated were less likely to say they would. "This finding tends to support the bulk of work dedicated to prison culture and sexual assault, where inmate reports to staff could add additional consequences, like retaliation or additional labels of being 'weak,' which could lead to increased harassment by other inmates," the authors write.

Black inmates were 13.7 percent more likely than white inmates to say they would report their sexual assault. On the other hand, prisoners who had served more time were less likely to say they'd report. "For every year served, there is a 2.7 percent decrease in the likelihood that an inmate would self-report her or his own victimization," the authors write.

Inmates who completed high school were 29.3 percent less likely than inmates who didn't finish high school to say they would report. Older inmates were more likely to say they'd report their assault.

The researchers also found that male inmates were 81 percent less likely than female inmates to recommend that a fellow prisoner report their assault to prison authorities. Also, those who said they knew someone who had been assaulted within the past year were twice as likely to say they would recommend reporting compared to inmates who knew no one who'd been victimized in the past year.

Other resources that may [be] helpful to journalists:

- The National Sexual Violence Resource Center is a leading source of data and information about sexual violence. RAINN, or the Rape, Abuse & Incest National Network, is an anti-sexual violence organization that operates the National Sexual Assault Hotline.
- The Prison Rape Elimination Act of 2003 requires states to implement a zero-tolerance policy for sexual assault within correctional facilities. It also requires the federal Bureau of Justice Statistics (BJS) to track and analyze the incidence of prison rape annually. The BJS provides a variety of related reports on its website.
- A 2017 study published in the academic journal PLOS One finds that 22 percent of all college students have experienced sexual assault but that women and gender non-conforming students are much more likely than men to say they have been assaulted. The study finds that 28 percent of women, 12 percent of men and 38 percent of transgender and other gender non-conforming students said they experienced at least one sexual assault while in college. It also finds that "freshman year, particularly for women, is when the greatest percentage experience an assault."
- A 2001 report commissioned by the American Association of University Women Educational Foundation, "Hostile Hallways: The AAUW Survey on Sexual Harassment in America's Schools," found that sexual harassment is common in public middle schools and high schools and that only four in 10 teenagers said they would likely complain to an adult if it happened to them.
- This annual report from the US Department of Defense, released in May 2018, shows the department "received

6,769 reports of sexual assault involving service members as either victims or subjects of criminal investigation, a 9.7 percent increase over the 6,172 reports made in fiscal 2016." All four military services—the U.S. Army, Navy, Air Force and Marine Corps—saw increases in reporting.

12

The Real Problem Is Male Violence and the Patriarchy

M. K. Fain

M. K. Fain is an engineer and writer with a background in grassroots activism, focusing on animal liberation, feminism, and software freedom. She is a writer and editor for Women's Way, a nonprofit organization empowering organizations and individuals to take action to support equal opportunity for women, girls, and gender equality for all.

After the initial shock and momentum of the #MeToo Movement, it may appear that the universe finally is weeding out the "bad" guys. But what if the problem isn't just about individual offenders and instead is about an entire culture or way of life? This viewpoint author believes the problem lies with male violence and that the problem is a social one, not a personal one. Instead of some men insisting they are "good guys," and allies to women, we need to spotlight the fact that the patriarchy is complicit in violence against women.

We are currently two years into the #MeToo movement against sexual harassment, which continues to spread and take down powerful politicians, actors and comedians, and even clergymen. Even Joe Biden, a long time advocate for women's rights and policies such as the Violence Against Women Act, is facing his inevitable #MeToo moment. While it can be hard to measure, I would personally venture to say that overall the movement has succeeded in increasing awareness of the prevalence of sexual assault and harassment in the workplace, empowering survivors to speak up, and demonstrating a social intolerance to these specific behaviors—which is perhaps unprecedented.

It seems like all our faves are problematic, from Morgan Freeman to Ryan Seacrest. But while we are at the height of Call-Out-And-Cancel Culture with individual men facing accountability for their actions, the conversation does not seem to be moving beyond the wrongdoings of these famous men to the systemic issues at play. The over 250 men accused since 2017 span the political spectrum from Roy Moore, George H. W. Bush, Alex Jones, Brett Kavanaugh, and President Trump to Aziz Ansari, Al Franken, Wayne Pacelle, Justin Trudeau, and Vice President Biden—many of whom have even claimed to be feminists themselves. The buzz around every new accusation feels more like celebrity gossip at this point than any real demand for change.

What is missing from the #MeToo conversation is what feminists have been saying for over a century: the problem isn't just a few bad actors, it's male violence.

Before the protests of #NotAllMen and that women can be abusive too, let's consider the facts:

- 90% of perpetrators of sexual violence against women are men[1]
- 93% of perpetrators of sexual violence against men are men[1]
- 95% of perpetrators of all child sexual abuse are men[2]

The exact numbers may change overtime with each new study and methodology, but the pattern is always the same: men are overwhelmingly the perpetrators of sexual violence. Among perpetrators of sexual violence against lesbians, where you may expect more female offenders, males were still responsible for 89% of offenses, and 95% of sexual coercion of bisexual women involves a male perpetrator. In the one study I could find which looked at the gender of perpetrators of sexual assault against trans-identifying individuals (an issue with a serious dearth of research), the perpetrator was male 79% of the time.

Despite the crushing evidence that the sexual assault in our communities is part of a systemic pattern of male violence, including domestic violence and other forms of global violence against women, the #MeToo conversation is continually framed around individual men. This gives men who have not been accused of misconduct the ability to see themselves as "one of the good guys," "an ally to women," and even "feminists." And perhaps worst of all, women are buying it.

This is why we remain constantly disappointed in all our favorite male stars, and why our male friends, coworkers, husbands, and brothers are let off for their own misogyny: "I know him, he's a feminist and has always supported me! He wouldn't do this."

The truth is, yes he would. While men may not be born rapists who are incapable of overcoming their base desires, they are born into a world which teaches men that they have a right to the exact pleasure they desire, and are specifically owed it by women. While some men have been actively challenging this patriarchal notion and working to overcome their socialization, this is still the baseline socialization that boys in our society receive. There is no such thing as a "good man" or a "bad man"—there are just men who fall somewhere on a spectrum of how much violence they have enacted against women.

Take for example this woman, whose series of tweets recounting stories in which men did not rape her went viral:

> *I went out drinking with girl friends at a bar a few years later. I was flirting with a guy there, he grabbed my hand, pulled me outside, into an alley, he kissed me hard and then looked at me and said, "yes?" I didn't say anything.*
>
> *He said "go back inside then," maybe he was annoyed but he meant it, I went back inside. There wasn't a rapist at that bar.*

There's a lot to dissect here. For one, whether this particular man was a rapist or not, this woman really has no idea if there was a rapist at the bar that night. In fact in a room of even 10 men, it's incredibly likely that there were rapists there—considering that 31.7% of college-aged men in one study admitted that they would rape a woman if there were no consequences (and really, what consequences are there when only .5% of perpetrators serve jail time?). One study found that 35% of college-aged men had committed one sexual assault since the age of 14. It's understandable that women may want to deny this. The truth that one in three men are rapists is not pleasant, and doesn't lend itself to feeling particularly safe around the men we have to interact with on a daily basis.

Further, the idea that because the man at the bar chose not to rape her he must therefore be one of the "good guys," fuels the misguided notion that men who are caught perpetrating violence against women are categorically different from those who aren't. Never-mind the fact that this man did actually grab her, separate her from her friends, and kiss her—all prior to gaining consent for any of these actions. While he decided against pulling the trigger on full-blown rape, his actions do display male-pattern sexual entitlement.

I know firsthand the fine line between a good man and a rapist. In 2015, I was sexually assaulted at a holiday party by someone who had been my friend since high school. This man had defended me against my abusive ex, was an elementary school teacher in an impoverished West Philly school, had travelled overseas to Georgia to teach English, and most strikingly—was an outspoken feminist. Yet it only took a bottle of wine (or two) for him to get a little rape-y. He later apologized to me, and promised to learn from his mistake and do better in the future. I do believe that apology and intent to learn was genuine, but nonetheless he is a perpetrator of sexual assault. Is this a good or bad man?

"Male violence is the worst problem in the world."

To say that the men who are publicly accused are no different from the yet un-accused is in no way an excuse for the violent and abhorrent behavior of sexual assault. Rather, it's time that women who want to see real change in the #MeToo era name the problem at hand. Sexual assault isn't an issue with Hollywood, the Catholic church, or R&B artists. As feminists have known for years: the issue is male-pattern violence, and sexual assault is only one facet of this violence which keeps women in a subservient class to men. Male violence extends beyond just sexual assault and abuse against women at home. Male violence is also war, mass shootings, gang violence … literally every form of measured violent crime. Many of these forms of violence compound, such as women and girls of ethnic and religious minorities in conflict regions being at heightened risk of sexual violence as a war tactic, according to the UN.

As the Huffington Post put it, "Male violence is the worst problem in the world."

While we all have men in our lives that we love, acknowledging that men as a class are the oppressors of women as a class is necessary in not only ending sexual assault, but all forms of male supremacy. Viewing some men as the good guys who "would never" erases the material reality of the condition of women compared to that of men. The patriarchy is something all men are complicit in to some degree, just as all white people have been complicit in white supremacy.

The modern feminist movement, in which you can claim you are a feminist by simply believing in equality, has been eager to include men under the label. Emma Watson's #HeForShe typifies this phenomenon. But as Al Jazeera pointed out in July, "the problem of male entitlement and misogynist attitudes towards women is a social one, not a personal one, and certainly not one that will be resolved by more men insisting they are feminists."

Rather than letting the very class that is oppressing us into the movement and scapegoating a few "bad apples" on Twitter, the mainstream feminist movement needs to come to terms with the pervasive reality of male violence. Nearly every adult male will commit some form of sexual violence against women, even if they never commit criminal sexual assault—whether it is through buying sex (20%), sexual harassment at work (33%), viewing pornography (98%), campus sexual assault (35%), coercing a woman into certain sex acts (46% of college men), or simply maintaining the systems that allow this to happen.

Ending sexual assault is about more than consent education and cancelling abusive men. We must demand an end to the acceptance of violent male sexuality, support feminist spaces for women to organize without men pretending to be allies for their own gain, and consider the global unionization of women against all forms of sexual exploitation. This Sexual Assault Awareness Month, I challenge feminists to name the problem. Let's hold men accountable for male violence, and demand an end to this epidemic of global terrorism against women. In doing so, we become that much closer to toppling the pillars of patriarchy.

Notes

1. https://www.cdc.gov/violenceprevention/pdf/nisvs_report2010-a.pdf
2. https://www.inspq.qc.ca/en/sexual-assault/fact-sheets/sexual-assault-women#ref

13

Can You Count On the Courts?

Alesha Durfee

Alesha Durfee is Associate Professor of Women and Gender Studies at Arizona State University. Her research and teaching focus on domestic violence, social policy, and structural intersectionality, including mandatory arrest policies and civil protection orders. She currently has a Researcher-Practitioner Partnership grant from the National Institue of Justice to study institutional and contextual factors that influence protection order filing and issuance rates using both quantitative and qualitative data.

This viewpoint focuses on the story of a case involving Virginia Lieutenant Governor Justin Fairfax to explain why many sexual assault victims do not come forward to report their experiences, particularly when the abuser is in the public eye. Because the burden of proof is on sexual assault victims, their claims often are not believed because there are no witnesses or no hard proof to corroborate them. Knowing the difficulty they will face, the victims therefore may feel it is not worth the emotional trauma to report their assaults. But women have a duty to bring sexual abusers to justice, and so it is the system that must be changed.

"Latest Allegations of Sexual Assault Show How the Legal System Discourages Victims from Coming Forward," by Alesha Durfee, The Conversation, 02/11/2019. https://theconversation.com/latest-allegations-of-sexual-assault-show-how-the-legal-system-discourages-victims-from-coming-forward-111406. Licensed under CC BY-ND 4.0 International.

Virginia's Lt. Gov. Justin Fairfax is refusing to resign after denying charges by two women who have said that he sexually assaulted them.

The first woman to come forward was Vanessa Tyson, a politics professor at Scripps College. She initially contacted *The Washington Post* after Fairfax's election in December 2017, alleging that Fairfax forced her to perform oral sex in 2004.

The *Post* stated it did not publish a story at that time because it "could not corroborate Tyson's account or find similar complaints of sexual misconduct."

So Tyson's story did not make national headlines until this week, when it was first published by the conservative blog Big League Politics.

The second woman to come forward is Meredith Watson, who alleges Fairfax raped her while they were both students at Duke University in 2000. According to a statement written by her attorneys, Watson told a dean at the school about the rape, and the dean "discouraged her from pursuing the claim further."

On Feb. 9, Fairfax asked the FBI to investigate their allegations. While it's not clear that the FBI will investigate, the controversy raises important questions about how the legal system deals with cases of sexual assault.

I am a scholar of domestic and sexual violence, and my work has focused on analyzing the stories survivors share when they seek safety and hold perpetrators accountable for abuse. I've also studied what happens when the legal system encounters and processes these stories.

What I've found is a fundamental mismatch between what survivors disclose and what legal systems need to hear to take action.

Survivors and Systems Unaligned

Survivors of sexual assault expect to be able to share what they have experienced in a way that reflects how they have made sense of the event and its aftermath.

In contrast, courts want a report that is linear, providing an almost objective, dispassionate accounting of abuse with specific names, dates and "facts." They want independent evidence of the abuse.

The problem is, acts of sexual and domestic violence rarely occur in front of other people, and survivors of sexual and domestic violence often have little external evidence of their assault other than their story.

The end result is that systems that are supposed to help are, in general, unable to adequately assess and respond to survivors' stories.

For example, officers responding to cases of domestic violence often do not make arrests, especially in cases of sexual violence.

In an analysis of FBI data, my colleague Matthew Fetzer and I found that only 26 percent of cases of sexual domestic violence reported to the police resulted in an arrest (in comparison to 52 percent of cases of physical domestic violence).

This may be due to the intimate nature of sexual violence and the difficulty of proving sexual assault. As one woman who experienced sexual violence told researchers: "I was raped by my husband. There was no evidence except for bruises on the inside of my legs or the pain on my breasts, and you just can't prove it."

Many institutions and organizations make decisions based on stereotypes about survivors that rarely reflect their actual circumstances. That's especially true with survivors who are not "good victims," who are not white, middle-class women, and who do not have external documentation of their abuse.

For many survivors—especially women of color, women reporting violence committed by perpetrators who hold power or women who experience sexual violence—it's easier and safer to not report the abuse and pretend that the resulting trauma never happened.

To an outsider, the choice not to report an assault in the moment, or even years later, does not make sense.

They do not understand how survivors compartmentalize in order to survive or even thrive.

Many legal options for reporting sexual assault—such as calling the police—aren't designed with survivors' goals, needs and motivations in mind. So survivors do not see reporting as an option, and do not see the legal system as a resource.

Expecting a survivor to disclose their abuse to someone in the moment does not reflect current knowledge and theory about sexual and domestic assault.

Rethinking Responses to Violence

The Fairfax story is an opportunity to rethink how to help survivors of violence and how to hold perpetrators accountable for their actions.

In the right environment and with the right support, survivors will want to come forward, share their stories, and gain strength from doing so.

However, the legal system is an adversarial system with confusing and complex bureaucratic procedures and often untrained staff. As trauma scholar Dr. Judith Herman explains, "If one set out intentionally to design a system for provoking symptoms of traumatic stress, it might look very much like a court of law."

Survivors are asked to recall specific details about their victimization that they have repressed in order to survive. As one advocate said to me in an interview, "They're trying to forget what happened and here I am, asking them to write down, with as many details as they can, what they went through."

How might we create a more responsive system?

First: Stop requiring survivors to narrate their abuse. It's more detrimental than helpful, especially if we simply discount it as a "story" afterward.

If there is some form of external documentation, survivors should be able to provide that instead. If there is no external documentation, then the narrative should be elicited in a supportive environment of the survivor's choosing, with trained staff available to help them better understand the kinds of information that judges and law enforcement need.

Second: People charged with listening and responding to survivors need to be educated about the dynamics of domestic and sexual violence. While some are, many do not fully understand the ways in which domestic and sexual violence affect survivors. It is impossible for them to hear and respond appropriately unless they understand those dynamics.

Finally: Explore what believing and supporting a survivor means.

While the words "I believe" and "I support" are critically important, they should not become buzzwords that replace actions. When you believe a survivor and decide to support that survivor, you must act. You must make hard, even unpopular, decisions.

You must work to adapt the system in order to uphold justice.

I believe. Period. I believe.

14

Consent Cannot Be Present When There Is a Power Imbalance

Jesse Rifkin

Jesse Rifkin has been a staff writer for GovTrack Insider since 2016, focusing primarily on bill summaries. His writings on politics and other subjects have been published in the Washington Post, Politico Magazine, Los Angeles Times, USA Today, Daily Beast, *HuffPost Politics,* Hartford Courant, *and* Billboard.

It may seem obvious to make the assertion that law enforcement officers should not be allowed have sexual relations with people whom they are holding in their custody. Not only does this happen, however, but there is a loophole that can make it legal. About one in six law enforcement officers charged with sexual assault between 2006 and 2016 were let off the hook by claiming the sex they had with people in their custody was consensual. The truth is, of course, since there is a power imbalance in such situations, even if sex is consensual, it constitutes an abuse of power.

Should police officers or law enforcement officers be allowed to have sex with somebody in their custody—even if both parties consent?

"Closing the Law Enforcement Consent Loophole Act Would Jail Cops Who Have Sex with Someone in Their Custody," by Jesse Rifkin, Medium, August 30, 2018. https://govtrackinsider.com/closing-the-law-enforcement-consent-loophole-act-would-jail-cops-who-have-sex-with-someone-in-their-78b8d11c2804. Licensed under CC BY 4.0.

Context

About one out of six law enforcement officers charged with sexual assault between 2006 and 2016 were either acquitted or had the charges dropped by acknowledging the sex but claiming it was consensual.

The federal government allows consent to be used as a defense when law enforcement officials acknowledge having sex with somebody in protective custody. More than half the states allow the consent defense as well.

The issue gained national attention after a viral article from BuzzFeed News in February about an 18-year-old woman who alleged that two Brooklyn police detectives raped her while in their police van. The two detectives acknowledge there was sex, but say it was consensual.

(Both detectives have resigned from the narcotics force on which they served due to public pressure and negative attention, even as they both claim innocence ahead of their upcoming trial.)

What the Bill Does

The Closing the Law Enforcement Consent Loophole Act [H.R. 6568] would make it a crime for a federal law enforcement officer to have sex with anybody in their custody and prohibit a claim of consensual sex as a defense.

Anybody found guilty would face up to 15 years in prison for the act—even if all participants stated that it was consensual.

Federal law enforcement officers include anybody with Immigrations and Customs Enforcement (ICE), the FBI, Department of Homeland Security, and other similar organizations.

The bill would also incentivize the 31 states which still allow the practice to change their state law and encourage annual reports to Congress reporting the number of such complaints, by providing additional funding to states that do so through the Violence Against Women Act.

The bill was introduced in late July by Rep. Jackie Speier (D-CA14).

What Supporters Say

Supporters argue the bill criminalizes an action that should clearly be criminal: raping somebody while in a position of legal power over them, then falsely claiming it was consensual.

"Though New York has since closed its ludicrous loophole, a staggering 31 states still allow law enforcement officers to claim that a sexual encounter with someone in their custody was consensual to avoid criminal charges," Rep. Speier said in a press release. "There is also no federal law that eliminates the consent defense for federal law enforcement, with the exception of federal corrections employees."

"And research shows that sexual misconduct is the second most frequently reported form of police abuse, yet the true scope of the problem is unknown because states are not required to report these kinds of allegations or arrests to the Bureau of Justice Statistics."

"This is unconscionable. Law enforcement members wield incredible power in their ability to detain individuals," Rep. Speier continued. "Our bill ensures that police will act accordingly in their official duties, as befitting their role as officers of the law, and that any such abuse of this power will not be tolerated."

What Opponents Say

GovTrack Insider was unable to locate any outright statements of opposition to the legislation, likely due to the bad optics of such a public stance.

Recent equivalent state level measures passed unanimously in Maryland, Kansas, and New York. It also passed in New Hampshire on a voice vote with no recorded opposition.

Odds of Passage

The bill has one cosponsor across the aisle: Rep. Barbara Comstock (R-VA10). It awaits a potential vote in the House Judiciary Committee.

Even if the federal legislation doesn't pass or receive a vote, the issue is gaining momentum in the states. Since the BuzzFeed news article in February, four states from across the political spectrum—Kansas, Maryland, New Hampshire, New York—have banned all law enforcement officials from having sex with somebody in their custody.

15

Consent Requires an Equal and Mutually Satisfying Relationship

Dr. Gemma McKibbin

Dr. Gemma McKibbin is Research Fellow, Department of Social Work, School of Health Sciences, Faculty of Medicine, Dentistry and Health Sciences at the University of Melbourne.

All too accepted in western culture is the idea that a teacher and student can have a legitimate "love affair." Even if the teacher waits until the student reaches the age of consent to engage in sexual activity, and even if the union culminates in legitimate marriage, the relationship is always tainted by a power imbalance. Far from falling in love with someone who just happens to be underage and cultivating a healthy relationship, the teacher is in fact grooming a child for sex.

If you're a fan of podcasts, like I am, you've probably listened to The Teacher's Pet.

The chart-topping Australian investigative podcast explores the disappearance and alleged murder of Sydney mother Lynette Dawson by her husband Chris Dawson in 1982.

The Teacher's Pet, which was created and produced by journalist Hedley Thomas and Slade Gibson for *The Australian*,

"A Teacher's Pet or a Victim of Sexual Abuse?" by Dr. Gemma McKibbin, Pursuit, November 7, 2018. https://pursuit.unimelb.edu.au/articles/a-teacher-s-pet-or-a-victim-of-sexual-abuse. Licensed under CC BY-ND 3.0 AU.

has captivated millions of listeners around the world as it unearthed new evidence and witnesses in the unsolved 36-year-old cold case.

Importantly, it also drew attention to Chris Dawson's alleged perpetration of domestic violence against his wife and sparked interest in the ongoing investigation which Lyn's family hopes will flush out the evidence that might finally solve the case.

The podcast has also led to the welcome establishment of Strike Force Southwood—investigating historic claims of teachers systematically grooming teen students for sex at three Sydney high schools, including Cromer High, where Chris Dawson was a sports teacher.

It was here in the 1980s, that Chris Dawson began grooming then 16-year-old Joanne Curtis, who was a vulnerable school girl and a babysitter for the Dawson children. But she wasn't the only one.

Since the release of The Teacher's Pet earlier this year, a number of brave men and women have come forward to report past experiences of sexual abuse and exploitation perpetrated against them when they were students at Cromer, Forest and Beacon Hill high schools in NSW.

So, the podcast has done a lot of good and got potentially millions of people talking about some of the most difficult issues in our society.

But despite these important achievements, when I listened to the podcast, there was a problem.

At times, it uses language about sexual abuse and exploitation that's troubling. The language we use to talk about sexual abuse and how we describe is vitally important.

Chris Dawson's sexual abuse and exploitation of 16-year-old Joanne Curtis is often referred to as "an intense sexual relationship." A headline in *The Australian* reads "the footballer, his schoolgirl lover and the missing wife" while the story goes onto to describe Chris moving his "teenage lover" into the family home.

In the 1980s when Chris Dawson began to groom Joanne Curtis, the legal age of consent in NSW was 16.

This meant that 16-year-old Joanne Curtis could technically consent to sleeping with an adult. However, the NSW Crimes Act at the time had an offence known as Section 73—carnal knowledge by a teacher, which stated:

> *Whoever, being a schoolmaster or other teacher, or a father, or step-father, unlawfully and carnally knows any girl of or above the age of ten years, and under the age of seventeen years, being his pupil, or daughter, or step-daughter, shall be liable to penal servitude for fourteen years.*

Chris Dawson was Joanne Curtis's teacher at Cromer High. Under the law at the time, he was not allowed to have sex with her until she was 17 years of age, and ethically, probably never. So, rather than having an "intense sexual relationship," Chris Dawson sexually abused Joanne and then continued to exploit her vulnerability by offering a roof over her head in exchange for sex.

Sexual exploitation is a form of child sexual abuse that involves a perpetrator taking advantage of an imbalance of power to trap a young victim into sexual activity in exchange for something they want or need, like a place to live.

But it's also very common for victims not to recognise that they are being exploited at the time, and instead perceive themselves to be in a relationship with the person perpetrating the crime.

In fact, Professor Marcia Neave, who acted as Commissioner for Victoria's Royal Commission into Family Violence, recently described child sexual abuse as a "wicked problem" supported by a culture of denial and victim-blaming.

What's worrying is to hear such a popular podcast falling into the trap of using language that plays into this kind of culture, particularly in the wake of the national apology to survivors of child sexual abuse.

The Royal Commission into Institutional Responses to Child Sexual Abuse made significant inroads into disrupting the culture of denial and victim-blaming that has not only enabled, but also excused, child sexual abuse for too many decades. But, the language used in The Teacher's Pet to describe Chris Dawson's sexual abuse and exploitation of Joanne Curtis harks back to a pre-Royal Commission culture.

Whenever we discuss issues like this, we must be mindful to use language that supports the survivor and holds the perpetrator to account. Words like "abuse," "exploitation" and "victim"—not "relationship."

Joanne Curtis was not in an intense relationship with Chris Dawson at the age of 16. Chris Dawson sexually abused and exploited her. Being sexually abused is not the same as being in a relationship. Relationships are meant to be equal, respectful and mutually satisfying.

Suggesting 16-year-old Joanne had any agency in Chris Dawson's exploitation of her is profoundly dangerous and risks recreating the victim-blaming culture that the Royal Commission worked so hard to undo.

By today's standard, even after Joanne Curtis turned 17, we would understand her to be a victim of sexual exploitation and to require a therapeutic response. Sexual abuse and exploitation can skew children's emerging sexualities so that they think the exploitation is normal. This may be what happened to Joanne Curtis as she moved into early adulthood and was pressured by Chris Dawson to marry him.

And that's why it's so important to be aware of the way we describe sexual abuse.

I think we should come up with a new name for The Teacher's Pet podcast: "Chris Dawson's sexual abuse and exploitation of Joanne Curtis." It's not catchy, and it might be a bit long, but it's accurate.

Being a teacher's pet suggests innocence or Granny Smith apples on a desk. There's nothing innocent about sexually abusing and exploiting children and then blaming them for it.

Let's be careful about the language we use.

16

The Blurry Line on Campus

Tovia Smith

Tovia Smith is a National Public Radio correspondent based in Boston, Massachusetts, who has reported extensively on the #MeToo movement and campus sexual assault. She also has covered the sexual abuse scandal within the Catholic Church. Smith has won dozens of national journalism awards including numerous honors from the Corporation for Public Broadcasting, Public Radio News Directors Association, and the Associated Press.

Sexual consent is a particularly burning issue on college campuses. In this viewpoint, the author cites the steps being taken in various New England higher education institutions to make clearer what is perceived by some as a blurry line between sexual consent and unwanted sex. Smith interviewed a myriad of school officials who are on the front line of the battle to make their institutions safer. These practices might not be employed in "the real world" but they are an attempt to start conversations with young adults and make them aware of their choices and the consequences of their actions.

As the federal government presses colleges to improve the way they handle cases of sexual assault, schools are turning their focus to defining "consent"—how to distinguish between activity that's consensual and activity that's not.

On one level, it's obvious. As the old line goes, "You know it when you see it." But less obvious is how to spell it out for the student handbook. There are about as many different definitions of consent as there are colleges.

"If consent were easy to put into words, we'd have a sentence, and we wouldn't have a page and a half of definition," says Mary Spellman, dean of students for Claremont McKenna College, which recently rewrote its definition.

As with most colleges, the bulk of Claremont McKenna's definition covers what's not consent. That's the easier part. For example, any OK from someone who's drunk or drugged or coerced can never count as consent. And consent to have sex last weekend or even an hour ago can't imply consent now.

But the definition also tries to get at those grayer areas, like when a student may be ambivalent or when something ends up happening that a student never intended.

Claremont McKenna's definition says permission has to be "clear, knowing and voluntary," but it also has to be "active, not passive." So a student who's silent, for example—or not resisting—is by definition not consenting.

"I don't think [the definition] is perfect," Spellman says. "I think it's come a long way, but I think we will find over time that it will evolve."

Only "Yes" Means "Yes"

The trend now, and what the White House recommended in its recent guidance to colleges, is toward what's called "affirmative consent." In other words, instead of the old "no means no," the idea now is that only "yes means yes."

But even that still leaves room for interpretation—or misinterpretation—since "yes" can be expressed nonverbally.

"Is the person actively participating?" says Spellman. "Are they touching me when I am touching them? Are they encouraging me when I'm doing various different things? Those would all be signs that the person is an active participant in whatever is going on."

To try to make it a little more clear, some schools amend their definitions with a series of explicit scenarios that read like sexual consent word problems. Yale offers two pages of them.

In one example, "Tyler and Jordan are both drinking heavily ... Tyler becomes extremely drunk. Jordan offers to take Tyler home ... [and] ... initiates sexual activity ... Tyler looks confused and tries to go to sleep. Jordan has sex with Tyler."

Yale prints the answer in italics: *"There was no consent to have sex ... The penalty would be expulsion."*

But other examples are trickier. One describes two friends, Morgan and Kai, who are engaging in sexual activity in Kai's room. Morgan "looks up at Kai questioningly" before escalating the activity and "Kai nods in agreement" so Morgan proceeds. But when Kai reciprocates, "Morgan lies still for a few minutes, then moves away, saying it is late and they should sleep."

On that one, Yale says that Kai wrongly assumed that it was OK to reciprocate *"but took no steps to obtain unambiguous agreement. The ... penalty would likely be a reprimand."*

"When you see these scenarios, you understand that this is something that is complicated," says Rory Gerberg, a student at Harvard's Kennedy School of Government who helped advise the White House on its recent guidance for schools. She says these kinds of hypotheticals are critical to showing students what "loud and clear" consent actually looks like.

Carefully crafted legal definitions are one thing, Gerberg says, "but knowing what that actually means in their life on a Friday or Saturday night is different."

A clear definition is critical not only to educate students, but also for the adjudication process. Just ask Djuna Perkins, a former prosecutor who now consults with colleges as an investigator of complaints and is the one left trying to sort through the murky question of whether a student's actions amounted to a nonverbal "yes."

"The fact of the matter is that consent is very tricky, and you're getting into minutiae of what happened in a particular event," she says. "It will sometimes boil down to details like who turned who around, or [whether] she lifted up her body so [another student] could pull down her pants.

"There have been plenty of cases that I've done when the accused student says, 'What do you mean? [The accuser] was moaning with pleasure. He was raising his body, clutching my back, exhibiting all signs that sounded like this was a pleasurable event.'"

Perkins says schools are being asked to define consent more narrowly than even most state criminal laws do. And the stakes couldn't be higher; those who get it wrong risk not only lawsuits and bad press, but also the loss of federal funding. The federal government is already investigating at least 55 schools for complaints that they're too soft on sexual assault.

"Some [schools] feel like they want to throw up their hands," Perkins says. "I know of colleges who are trying to revise their policies literally every summer. In this climate, I don't think there's a single school out there that really, truly feels like it's under control."

Antioch's Approach

Some schools have tried to avoid the ambiguity by mandating that students get explicit verbal permission before making any sexual advance. (The only way around the rule is if students have a prior verbal agreement to use a pre-arranged hand signal.)

"It's on them to say, 'Can I do this?' And the person has to respond verbally, 'Yes.' And if they don't, it's considered nonconsent, and that's a violation of our policy," says Louise Smith, dean of community life at Antioch College.

Smith says consent by Antioch's definition has to be clear and enthusiastic. "I guess so" wouldn't cut it. Also, the Antioch definition says consent must be continually renewed each time things escalate to "each new level of sexual activity."

The policy actually goes back to the early 1990s, when it was seen as so extreme it was mocked on *Saturday Night Live.*

"Yeah, we're not laughing now," says Smith. She says Antioch feels vindicated because the rest of the country is finally coming around.

Smith says students are also beginning to realize that getting verbal consent doesn't have to be awkward or a mood killer.

"Yeah, it can be hot, like, 'Do you like it when I bite your neck?'" says Rebecca Nagle, co-founder of a group called Force: Upsetting the Culture of Rape, which runs campus workshops and a website using the slogan "Consent Is Sexy."

"We can be making out, and I can be like, 'So, how do you feel about teeth?'" Nagle says. "And if I have a certain look in my eye, that's really flirty. And then, I can be like, 'Do you like it like this?' And that exchange is incredibly hot," she says.

Nagle says students are starting to understand that it's better to deal with asking—even if it does feel forced—than with a morning-after accusation that the sex was nonconsensual. But as others see it, colleges are overstepping by trying to script what students should say in the dark of their dorm rooms and by imposing an unfair standard.

"Students will have their lives maybe seriously damaged by administrators who are essentially creating standards by the seat of their pants," says Anne Neal, president of the American Council of Trustees and Alumni. She worries that the stricter standards come with no due process for the accused, who face the burden of proving they did have enthusiastic and continual consent.

Neal says allegations of sexual assault should be handled by the criminal justice system, not schools. "To allow bureaucrats on our college campuses arbitrarily to determine what is consent and what is not, when even the law has difficulty, certainly underscores the absurdity of this system," she says.

But pressure on colleges is only increasing, both from the government and from their own students.

Murylo Batista, a junior at Dartmouth College, has been pressing his school to narrow its definition of consent. He says he's shocked by how many students still don't get it and are unsure the morning after if they crossed the line.

"That freaks me out!" he says. "How do you not know if you raped someone or not? That is pretty scary to me."

Batista says colleges are not the only ones who have to do more to help young people understand the meaning of consent. In order for students to really get it, he says, the lesson needs to start long before students even get to college.

17

Learning Consent in College

Mary Kate Leahy

Mary Kate Leahy is an Issue Brief Specialist at Law Street Media. She has a J.D. from William and Mary and a Bachelor's in Political Science from Manhattanville College. She is also a proud graduate of Woodlands Academy of the Sacred Heart.

The frequency of sexual violence on college campuses is cited by the author the following viewpoint. Mary Kate Leahy uses statistics to point out that many attacks on campus go unreported for a myriad of reasons, including that both the perpetrators and victims are often in the same social circle. She writes also about affirmative consent, which necessitates an explicit agreement to engage in sexual activity from both partners, rather than a presumption of consent unless it is denied expressly.

When most people think about rape and sexual violence they imagine a situation where a woman is attacked by a man she does not know. We usually do not think of college campuses, particularly dating on college campuses, as a place where rape is likely to occur. Yet college campuses are a dangerous place for both female and male students and the rate of rape and sexual violence is startling. During their college years, one in five women are sexually assaulted or raped. And it is not just female students who are victimized, as 17 percent of student victims are male.

"College Campuses and the Role of Affirmative Consent," by Mary Kate Leahy, Law Street Media, LLC., December 5, 2016. Reprinted by permission of Fastcase.com, Inc.

Rapes on college campuses do not fit our mental model for how rape occurs, which makes it difficult to combat and makes victims reticent to report crimes. Among college women, nine out of 10 knew their rapist. Rape is particularly likely for freshmen and sophomores, especially cases of incapacitated rape, which happens to 15 percent of female freshmen.

Reporting Problems

Despite high rates of violence, only 20 percent of victims report the crime to the police. There are multiple reasons why victims may not choose to go to the police. Oftentimes the victim and the rapist are in the same social circle and victims fear social reprisal for reporting. They may also fear that their claims will not be taken seriously by the police or school officials and that they may be subject to disciplinary action or criminal prosecution themselves. Remember, many of these victims have been drinking underage and/or using drugs prior to their rape.

Victims may also have been conditioned to think that their rape was not a "real" rape. Their rapist is someone that they know, not a stranger grabbing them in a dark alley. Force may not have been used since often the victim was incapacitated at the time. Our culture also offers multiple excuses for rapists and puts blame on victims who were intoxicated or otherwise "irresponsible." These feelings of guilt on the part of the victim are internalized and expressed by not reporting the crime because it isn't worth dealing with.

In an effort to combat the problem of rape on campus, many colleges and universities have adopted affirmative consent practices. The use of affirmative consent to change cultural attitudes about rape and/or to change rules on how to prosecute sexual violence has caused a great deal of controversy and should be more thoroughly examined.

What Is Affirmative Consent?

For a full background on rape culture and affirmative consent, you can read this article: https://lawstreetmedia.com/issues/law-and-politics/rape-culture-theory-consent/. So let's unpack some of the arguments surrounding affirmative consent. Jaclyn Friedman, the affirmative consent advocate, explains that the "no-means-no" standard (where consent is presumed unless it is expressly denied) doesn't deal well with some kinds of sexual assault. In particular, it does not provide adequate protection from abuse for victims who may freeze up and feel too unsafe to deny consent. This is actually a common reaction, particularly for victims who are sexually inexperienced, incapacitated, or conditioned to not resist. When the burden is placed on all participants to make sure that everyone is consenting, it eliminates some of these dangers. It also would eliminate a situation where one party feels they were victimized and the other party honestly does not feel they did anything wrong because they thought silence was consent.

In a culture where silence indicates a lack of consent, not evidence of it, it becomes much more difficult for this to happen. This could be especially helpful for younger college students, or the sexually inexperienced, who are in fact more likely to be assaulted than their older student peers.

Shikha Dalmia takes a different view on the issue because of how affirmative consent changes the burden of proof and, in her view, the presumption of innocence. Her main objection is not that we may want to adopt this as a cultural model for how consent works but that we might use affirmative consent as a legal framework. As she states, consent is already required, under the "no-means-no" standard. But we presume that there was consent until the non-initiator indicates otherwise. This presumption is necessary, in Dalmia's view, to maintain a presumption of innocence for those accused of rape.

We have to take that concern seriously because the presumption that everyone is innocent until proven guilty is a cornerstone of our judicial system. But changing the presumption of consent does not necessarily lead to a change in the burden of proof/presumption of innocence.

In a formal rape trial, the prosecution currently needs to show that the victim did not give consent, but that is not the same as saying we assume they are lying. In some instances where the defendant is asserting impotence or intoxication as a defense against rape they are already required to prove that element of the case, yet it does not change the underlying presumption of their innocence. Requiring one party to prove an element of the charge does not mean that we assume that party is being deceptive.

We are placing the burden of proof on the prosecution to prove a lack of consent. And they offer evidence for this such as the actions of the victim and defendant, including but not limited to what was said. But if consent was not presumed that wouldn't change the fact that we are still asking the prosecution to prove its case. Prosecutors would still have to contend with any evidence the defense offers to show that there was in fact consent, and they would still be offering their own evidence to show that nothing the victim did amounted to consent. It would change the understanding of what all parties should have understood at the time of the incident—that they should have obtained consent—not be a commentary on what the defendant did or did not do.

A Practical Solution?

The second problem is how affirmative consent actually works in practice. Is it really something that will "work" on campuses, or in the general population, given our cultural scripts for how men and women behave sexually?

There are impracticalities to the use of affirmative consent but not for the reasons that detractors might suggest. The impracticality is not in asking for consent during a sexual encounter. The main obstacle is changing the cultural norm so that not getting that consent is a problem.

But hasn't that been the case in all movements for increased social justice? Sharing a water fountain between blacks and whites was never impractical on its face, in fact, it is even more practical to have one water fountain. Just as affirmative consent as a model has the potential to reduce confusion and assault. The impracticality is from an unwillingness to implement a new system that changes social norms, gender norms in this case, not with the new norms themselves. There may not be enough evidence of how effective affirmative consent is on college campuses to draw a conclusion about its implementation. But there is some anecdotal evidence that even skeptics can incorporate affirmative consent into their sexual behavior.

[There is a] concern about the practicality of the system and the appropriateness of how affirmative consent policies have been added to most college campuses. Many of these institutions adopted an affirmative consent model because the Obama administration, as part of the "It's On Us" program, made continued federal funding contingent upon colleges dealing meaningfully with sexual assault.

Some of these objections are based on a misunderstanding, sometimes a deliberately created misunderstanding, of affirmative consent. It certainly does not require written consent, and in fact, does not require even verbal consent. Obviously, a written document would be your strongest piece of evidence in a case trying to show you had obtained consent. But that doesn't mean that it is the only way to do so, and this line of reasoning conflates the idea of how affirmative consent would work in practice in most sexual encounters with how affirmative consent might affect a legal proceeding.

What Affirmative Consent Would Change

Either at the school or the state level, a legal proceeding is only changed by explicit amendments to the burden of proof or the presumption of innocence. Affirmative consent does not do that. Our current prosecutorial system functions perfectly well, even when consent is at issue, without a document signed by the victim saying they didn't consent. There is no reason to think that a written contract would be required simply by asking an initiator to make sure their sexual activity was welcome.

In fact, if you look at one example definition of affirmative consent used by a university, specifically the State University of New York, it explicitly includes actions as one method to show consent. The key is that the words or actions create a "clear permission" regarding willingness.

But there is still discomfort with the idea that the federal government can influence policy at colleges around the country by threatening to withhold funding. Some people think it is inappropriate to try to strong arm a college in this way.

And yet the government already engages in this behavior all the time, in other contexts, to promote fair treatment. One example is the area of special education. While I was at William and Mary I worked in our clinic for children with special needs, ensuring that they received FAPE—a free and appropriate public education. In exchange for federal funding, the state of Virginia agreed to follow certain guidelines for how they were required to handle children with special needs. Before the implementation of the law that allowed this, the Individuals with Disabilities Education Act, children with special needs were often shoved into a corner and ignored.

Most people would not object to this requirement because they realize that sometimes you need practical reasons to encourage socially just behavior. As much as we would like to think otherwise, people do not always behave morally on their own, state governments and colleges included. The federal government has consistently used the power of the purse to encourage behavior to support marginalized groups. The fact that they are doing so now, to protect students from sexual assault, should not matter. A prudish or squeamish reaction to the involvement of the government in sexual matters focuses on the sex and not on the violence. Rape that occurs when someone is incapacitated, knows the attacker, was drinking, etc. is just as much an act of violence as a stranger jumping a victim on the street. And there is no more quintessentially appropriate role for government than the prevention of violence against its citizens.

Conclusion

We need to deal with rape as it actually happens in reality, rather than dealing with rape as it is portrayed in our culture. A rapist is not always, or even usually, a stranger. It does not always happen with physical violence; often sexual assault happens in a wider social context. And because sexual assault is inextricably linked with sexual conduct in general, we have to address our sexual culture if we want to address sexual assault.

Affirmative consent may not be a panacea for the issue of sexual assault, even just on college campuses. The use of alcohol and drugs, the tight-knit social communities where these assaults occur, and the relative sexual immaturity of the age group all make sexual assault more complicated on a college campus. But the discussion of whether we want to adopt this model, either in a social or in a judicial context, has opened the door for people to grapple with what consent really means. That discussion is a valuable one for us to be having.

18

Consent Is a Simple Matter

Paul Gowder

Paul Gowder is a law professor at the University of Iowa and a political scientist. He writes about constitutional law, political philosophy, data, professional ethics, and justice. He is a former civil rights and legal aid lawyer who represented victims of police misconduct, predatory lending, employment discrimination, unlawful eviction, domestic violence, and numerous other injustices.

The following viewpoint is a tongue-in-cheek argument expressed humorously that manages to explain sexual consent simply and clearly. The author uses the analogy of borrowing a friend's car under several different conditions to explain that it should actually be quite obvious when it is and when it is not acceptable to hold someone accountable to "consent"—whether it's consenting to loan a car or consenting to a sexual encounter.

Suppose I want to borrow a friend's car. So here's what I do: I wait till my friend gets really stinking drunk. Like, goofy drunk. I bring him a few more Bloody Marys to help it along. Then I half-walk, half-carry my drunk-ass friend home. When we get to his house, I let him in the door, and drag his unresisting drunk self over to the hook where he keeps the car keys. He's still in party mode. He's screaming "YEEAAAH!! BROOOO!" in response to basically everything I say. He can hardly stand up straight. I set him down on the couch and say "dude, you mind if I take these?" while pointing at the car keys. He's continuing to babble senselessly. I take the car and drive off.

Has he loaned me the car?

(Does it matter whether I was drunk too?)

Ok, now I want to borrow a different friend's car. And this friend doesn't drink. Woah, how am I going to get drove without the help of booze?

But, you know what, I have reason to believe this friend is a little timid. So what I do, is I invite myself over to his house. I knock on the door, he opens it, and I walk right in. He looks a little uncomfortable already, but I ignore that. Instead, I walk straight over to the car keys, and I take them. He starts to stammer out something like "what are you doing?" but I just talk over him. "I'm taking your car" I say, as I walk out the door. "Uuuhh," he starts to say, then falls silent. I take the car and drive off.

Has he loaned me the car?

Right. New friend, new car. This one is a bit more assertive, but a notoriously bad communicator. So I actually ask this time: "bro, can I borrow your car?" He says, "well, I'm not sure." I say, "dude, come on, just let me borrow your car." He says, "let me think about it." I say, "what's there to think about? I gotta have the car! What are you, some kind of tease?" He says, "maybe, gimme a minute to think." I take the car keys, walk out, and drive off.

Has he loaned me the car?

Ok, now I find another friend. And I actually ask that friend if I can borrow his car, when he's awake, and sober, and not currently being intimidated by anyone. And he says "yes." We didn't really talk about how long I could borrow the car for. It's the start of a three-day weekend. On Sunday night, my friend calls me up. "Buddy," he says, "I need the car back; my boss just said I've gotta go in to work tomorrow." "You tease," I say, "you can't just let me borrow the car and then take it back just when I'm starting to have fun driving it. I'm not finished with it." I keep the car for three more days.

For those last three days, has he loaned me the car?

I've got one friend left. (For some weird reason, none of the rest are talking to me.) Again, I actually ask this one if I can borrow the car, and he actually says "yes," and looks like he means it, and I drive off in it. I finish what I need to do, and I bring it back. I say "thanks man, you did me a solid." He says "no prob, anytime." The next day, when he's at work, I go back to his house, open the door, and take the car.

The second time around, has he loaned me the car?

If you know the answers to those questions, you understand the notion of affirmative consent.

Wouldn't it be weird if there was a special area of law where having that kind of consent rule was some kind of scary novelty that lots of people kick and scream and fight about?

Wouldn't it be even weirder if actual lawyers joined in the kicking and screaming and fighting, even though we have literally (not figuratively literally, actually literally literally) centuries of experience as a profession in determining whether people actually consented to something, even though we spend most of the first year in law school studying situations where consent is basically the whole question, even though the idea of affirmative consent, under its ordinary name, "consent," is shot through the whole Anglo-American common law tradition, from contract law to tort law to criminal law to property law, and even though in almost no situation in any of those fields "s/he didn't fight back" or "s/he didn't actually say no" or "I got him/her nice and drunk first" constitutes consent?

Yeah, I think so too.

Organizations to Contact

The editors have compiled the following list of organizations concerned with the issues debated in this book. The descriptions are derived from materials provided by the organizations. All have publications or information available for interested readers. The list was compiled on the date of publication of the present volume; the information provided here may change. Be aware that many organizations take several weeks or longer to respond to inquiries, so allow as much time as possible.

Battered Women's Justice Project
1801 Nicollet Ave. S., Suite 102
Minneapolis, MN 55403
(612) 824-8768
email: technicalassistance@bwjp.org
website: www.bwjp.org

The Battered Women's Justice Project promotes justice and safety for victims of intimate partner violence and works with other groups to provide assistance. The organizations help train professionals in the field to legally aid victims of such attacks. The Battered Women's Justice Project also advocates for victims through law enforcement, the courts, and the political process.

Center for Relationship Abuse Awareness
555 Bryant St., #272
Palo Alto, CA 94301
(800) 700-7233
website: www.stoprelationshipabuse.org

The Center for Relationship Abuse Awareness provides awareness and education for all involved in the problem, including communities, schools, and youth working in a collective effort to end gender violence. Among the goals is to prevent the blaming of victims and focus on punishing the perpetrators.

End Rape on Campus
1440 G St. NW
Washington, DC 20005
(202) 281-0323
email: info@endrapeoncampus.org
website: www.endrapeoncampus.org

End Rape on Campus works to stop campus violence through support of survivors and their communities, as well as prevention through education. The organization also works on policy reform at all levels, including on campus, while establishing support networks, filing complaints of sexual abuse, and monitoring student activities. Among its goals is to end the blaming of victims and focusing on punishing offenders.

Futures Without Violence
1320 19th St. NW, #401
Washington, DC 20036
(202) 595-7382
email: info@futureswithoutviolence.org
website: www.futureswithoutviolence.org

Futures Without Violence seeks to end sexual violence and other forms of violence through programs, policies, and campaigns that empower individuals, particularly women. Futures Without Violence trains healthcare professionals and those working with youth to improve responses to violence. It also advocates for victims through community leadership and education.

National Sexual Violence Resource Center
Governor's Plaza North, Bldg. 2
2101 North Front St.
Harrisburg, PA 17110
(877) 739-3895
website: www.nsvrc.org

The National Sexual Violence Resource Center is a nonprofit group that provides information and tools to prevent and respond to sexual violence. The organization uses research and follows trends to determine the most successful means to help individuals, communities, and service providers create change that will remain strong while responding effectively to sexual violence.

Rape, Abuse & Incest National Network (RAINN)
1220 L St. NW
Washington, DC 20005
(800) 656-4673
email: online.rain.org
website: www.rainn,org

RAINN is the largest anti-sexual violence organization in the United States. Among its benefits is the National Sexual Assault Hotline, which allows victims and others to report wrongdoing. The organization works with more than 1,000 local sexual abuse assault service providers to help survivors and work toward bringing perpetrators to justice.

United States Department of Justice
950 Pennsylvania Ave.
Washington, DC 20530-0001
(202) 514-2000
email: askovc@ncjrs.gov
website: www.justice.gov

The US Department of Justice is a government agency that works to identify and prevent bias in law enforcement in responding to sexual assault and domestic violence. Among its departments are the Office for Victims of Crime, Office on Violence Against Women, and Office on Sex Offender Sentencing, Monitoring, Apprehending, Registering, and Tracking (SMART).

Bibliography

Books

Laurie Halse Anderson, *Shout*. New York, NY: Viking Books for Young Readers, 2019.

Annie E. Clark and Andrea L. Pino, *We Believe You: Survivors of Campus Sexual Assault Speak Out*. New York, NY: Holt Paperbacks, 2016.

Mark Cowling, *Making Sense of Sexual Consent*. New York, NY: Routledge, 2016.

Cindy Crabb, *Learning Good Consent: On Healthy Relationships and Survivor Support*. Chico, CA: AK Press, 2016.

Joseph Fischel, *Sex and Harm in the Age of Consent*. Minneapolis MN: University of Minnesota Press, 2016.

Donna Freitas, *Consent on Campus: A Manifesto*. Oxford, UK: Oxford University Press, 2018.

Vanessa Grigoriadis. *Blurred Lines: Rethinking Sex, Power, and Consent on Campus*. New York. N.Y.: Eamon Dolan/ Mariner Books, 2018.

Kate Harding, *Asking for It: The Alarming Rise of Rape Culture— and What We Can Do About It*. Boston, MA: De Capo Lifelong Books, 2015.

Jennifer Lang, *Consent: The New Rules of Sex Education: Every Teen's Guide to Healthy Sexual Relationships*. San Antonio, TX: Althea Press, 2018.

Carla Mooney, *Everything You Need to Know About Sexual Consent*. New York, NY: Rosen Publishing, 2017.

New York Times Editorial, *#MeToo: Women Speak Out Against Sexual Assault*. New York, NY: New York Times, 2018.

Lori Perkins, *#MeToo: Essays About How and Why This Happened, What It Means, and How to Make Sure It Never Happens Again.* New York, NY: Riverdale Avenue Books, 2017.

Milena Popova, *Sexual Consent (MIT Press Essential Knowledge Series).* Cambridge, MA: MIT Press, 2019.

Chessy Prout and Jenn Abelson, *I Have the Right to: A High School Survivor's Story of Sexual Assault, Justice, and Hope.* New York, NY: Margaret K. McElderry Books, 2018.

Joyce Short, *Your Consent: The Key to Conquering Sexual Assault.* Amazon Digital Services, 2019.

Jennifer Yonker, *The Road to Healing: A Journal for Teen Survivors of Sexual Abuse.* CreateSpace Independent Publishing Platform, 2013.

Periodicals and Internet Sources

Lisa Feldman Barrett, "Why Men Need to Stop Relying on Non-Verbal Consent, According to a Neuroscientist," *Time*, May 11, 2018. http://time.com/5274505/metoo-verbal-nonverbal-consent-cosby-schneiderman/.

Berit Brogaard, "Why Agreement to Sex Is Not Consent," *Psychology Today*, March 31, 2018. https://www.psychologytoday.com/us/blog/the-mysteries-love/201803/why-agreement-sex-is-not-consent.

Nancy Brown, "Consent and Consensual Sex," Palo Alto Medical Foundation, October 2013. http://www.pamf.org/teen/abc/sex/consent.html.

Tara Culp-Ressler, "What 'Affirmative Consent' Actually Means," Think Progress, June 25, 2014. https://thinkprogress.org/what-affirmative-consent-actually-means-ea665b32b388/.

Amrit Dhillon, "Men Blame Women in Western Clothes: India's Rape Culture Is Thriving," *Sydney Morning Herald,* December 8, 2017. https://www.smh.com.au/world/lets-forget-what-we-said-five-years-ago-india-still-lives-with-a-rape-culture-20171207-h00ygg.html.

Grace Donnelly, "Anita Hill: Companies Should Treat Sexual Harassment as an Abuse of Power," *Fortune*, December 12, 2018. http://fortune.com/2018/12/12/anita-hill-sexual-harassment/.

Robyn Doolittle, "How Alcohol Complicates Sex Assault Cases," *Globe & Mail*, March 17, 2017. https://www.theglobeandmail.com/news/investigations/unfounded-too-drunk-to-consent-how-alcohol-complicates-sex-assault-cases/article34338370/.

"5 Things You Need to Know About Sexual Consent," Reach Out. https://au.reachout.com/articles/5-things-you-need-to-know-about-sexual-consent.

Donna Freitas, "Here's the Best Way to Start a Conversation with Young People About Sex and Consent," *Time*, September 21, 2018. http://time.com/5402048/sex-consent-college-students-ya-novels/.

Ellen Friedrichs, "5 Questions About Alcohol and Consent You're Too Afraid to Ask, Answered," Everyday Feminism, May 22, 2016. https://everydayfeminism.com/2016/05/alcohol-and-consent-questions/.

Megan Garber, "The Dangerous Insufficiency of 'No Means No,'" *The Atlantic,* August 1, 2018. https://www.theatlantic.com/entertainment/archive/2018/08/the-dangerous-insufficiency-of-no-means-no/566465/.

Anya Kamenetz, "Should We Teach About Consent in K-12? Brett Kavanaugh's Home State Says Yes," NPR, September 28, 2018. https://www.npr.org/2018/09/28/652203139/

should-we-teach-about-consent-in-k-12-brett-kavanaughs-home-state-says-yes.

Amee LaTour, "The Ins and Outs of Sexual Consent," Good Choices Good Life. http://www.goodchoicesgoodlife.org/ choices-for-young-people/the-ins-and-outs-of-sexual-consent/.

Simra Miriam, "'No Means No': It Really Is That Simple When It Comes to Consent," Huffington Post, August 1, 2017. https://www.huffpost.com/entry/no-means-no-it-really-is-that-simple-when-it-comes_b_598109b2e4b09d23 1a518252.

Charles G. Monnett III & Associates, "'No Means No'—Except in North Carolina," Carolina Law, August 8, 2018. https:// carolinalaw.com/blog/sexual-consent-law-north-carolina/.

Steven Petrow, "People Sre Talking About Sexual Consent. Would an App Help?" *USA Today*, February 20, 2018. https://www.usatoday.com/story/tech/ columnist/2018/02/20/sexual-consent-apps-set-rules-intimacy-come-their-own-risks/328635002/.

Stephanie Phillips, "Sexual Consent and the Law," The Mix, September 22, 2016. https://www.themix.org.uk/crime-and-safety/victims-of-crime/sexual-consent-and-the-law-18821. html.

Natalie Proulx, "What Constitutes Sexual Consent?" *New York Times*, May 16, 2018. https://www.nytimes.com/2018/05/16/ learning/what-constitutes-sexual-consent.html.

Lisa Rose, "Sexual Consent Is a Worldwide Conversation," CNN, April 5, 2018. https://www.cnn.com/2018/04/04/ world/consent-christiane-amanpour-sex-love-around-world/index.html.

Kalhan Rosenblatt, "'Consent at Any Age Is Consent': What Teenagers Think of the Kavanaugh Accusations—and His

Defenders," NBC News, September 26, 2018. https://www.nbcnews.com/news/us-news/consent-any-age-consent-what-teenagers-think-kavanaugh-accusations-his-n913266.

Katie Russell, "Rape and Consent: What You Need to Know Before You Have Sex," *The Independent*, November 3, 2015. https://www.independent.co.uk/life-style/love-sex/consent-rape-is-this-rape-a6718931.html.

"Sexual Abuse and Assault Against Women," WebMD. https://www.webmd.com/sexual-conditions/guide/sexual-abuse-and-assault#1.

Lourdes Avila Uribe, "These Are the Sad Reasons Many Women Don't Feel Comfortable Reporting Their Sexual Assault," Hello Giggles, April 26, 2017. https://hellogiggles.com/lifestyle/health-fitness/sad-reasons-women-dont-feel-comfortable-reporting-sexual-assault/.

"Was It Rape? Thinking About Consent and Unwanted Sex," Bedsider, September 12, 2017. https://www.bedsider.org/features/1080-was-it-rape-thinking-about-consent-and-unwanted-sex.

"What Is Consent? Healthy Relationships," Love Is Respect, https://www.loveisrespect.org/healthy-relationships/what-consent/.

Kathy Young, "Campus Rape: The Problem with 'Yes Means Yes,'" *Time*, August 29, 2014. http://time.com/3222176/campus-rape-the-problem-with-yes-means-yes/.

Index

5